SpeakEasy's

Survival Spanish For Educators

Myelita Melton, MA

SpeakEasy Communications, Inc.

Survival Spanish for Educators

Author: Myelita A. Melton, MA
Cover illustration: Ellen Wass Beckerman
Published by SpeakEasy Communications, Inc.
116 Sea Trail Drive
Mooresville, NC 28117-8493
USA

ISBN   0-9712593-5-6

Survival Spanish for Educators, SpeakEasy Spanish, SpeakEasy's Survival Spanish, SpeakEasy's Survival Spanish for Educators, and SpeakEasySpanish.com are either trademarks or registered trademarks of SpeakEasy Communications, Inc. in the United States and/or other countries.

The content of this book is furnished for informational use only, is subject to change without notice, and should not be construed as a commitment by SpeakEasy Communications, Incorporated. SpeakEasy Communications, Incorporated assumes no responsibility or liability for any errors, omissions, or inaccuracies that may appear in the informational content contained in this guide.

Foreword

I started learning Spanish at seventeen, and I think it's one of the best decisions I ever made. It happened by accident, but I don't think it was a coincidence. In my senior year of high school I just decided to take Spanish instead of Physics. The sciences were never my thing. On the first day of class, I was hooked. The sound of Spanish spoke to my soul, and I knew I had made the right decision. For the next year I begged my parents to let me take my savings and go to Mexico to study. They thought it was a crazy phase I was going through and it would pass eventually. It didn't. Three days after high school graduation I flew to Mexico for the first time. ¡Muchas gracias, Mom and Dad! Since high school, Spanish has always been a part of my life and it always will be. I'm glad that you are making Spanish a part of your life too.

Spanish hasn't always come easily to me. There have been plenty of times when I couldn't remember the right word— or any word for that matter. I've also made my share of mistakes, and I'm sure I always will. No matter what, I can say that knowing Spanish has rewarded me richly. It's brought me great friends I would never have had, and it's taken me places I would have never been brave enough to go. But best of all, it's given me a greater understanding of Latinos, the most fascinating people on our planet! So, this book is dedicated to you, one of the millions of Americans who want to reach out and make connections with neighbors, friends, colleagues, and customers who speak Spanish. I've loaded it with what I consider to be the essential things that hospitality and service industry professionals should know about one of the most beautiful and expressive languages in the world. ¡Buena suerte, amigos!

Lastly, I'd like to thank to my staff of instructors, proofreaders, artists and editors who catch my mistakes and continue to give me courage. Their time and talents are a constant blessing! Muchas gracias to Ellen Wass Beckerman, Elizabeth Stulz, Candice Tucker, Dr. Leslie Ahmadí, Dr. George Thatcher, Lisa Parker, and Alan Pickelsimer.

Survival Spanish for Educators
Table of Contents

Using This Material

Welcome to *SpeakEasy's Survival Spanish for Educators*™. This material is for adults with no previous experience in the Spanish language. Through research and interviews with professionals in your field, we have developed this material to be a practical guide to using Spanish on the job. Where ever possible, we have chosen to use the similarities between English and Spanish to facilitate your success.

Throughout the manual you will find study tips and pronunciation guides that will help you to say the words correctly. In the guides, we have broken down the Spanish words for you by syllables, choosing English words that closely approximate the Spanish sound needed. This makes learning Spanish more accessible because it doesn't seem so foreign. When you see letters that are **BOLD** in the guide, say that part of the word the loudest. The bold capital letters are there to show you where the emphasis falls in that particular word.

At SpeakEasy Communications, we believe that *communication* is more important than *conjugation*, and we urge you to set realistic, practical goals for learning. Make practice a regular part of your day and you will be surprised at the progress you make!

LATIN AMERICA

What's The Proper Term? Both!

Latino/Latina: Anyone from Latin America who speaks Spanish as his or her native language. (Preferred)

Hispanic: Anyone who speaks Spanish as his or her native language and traces family origin to Spain.

Note: Don't assume that because a person speaks Spanish that they are Mexican. They could be from anywhere in Latin America

Hispanics in America come mainly from the following three countries:

1. **Mexico**
2. **Cuba**
3. **Puerto Rico**

Many Latinos from El Salvador, Honduras and Guatemala are coming to America because of Hurricane Mitch in 1998.

According to US Census:

1. There are over 43 million in the US, who speak Spanish.
2. Hispanics are the majority minority in America.
3. By 2050 Hispanics will make up 25% of the US population.
4. Georgia & NC have the fastest growing Hispanic populations.
5. Over 17% of the nation's school-aged children are Latino.
6. Latino buying power surged this year to over 700 billion dollars. In 2007 it is expected to increase to over 900 billion dollars.
7. 47% are limited in English proficiency.

SpeakEasy's Secrets to Learning Spanish

Congratulations on your decision to learn to speak Spanish! This is one of the smartest choices you will ever make considering the increasing diversity in our country. It's definitely a decision you will never regret. You are now among a growing number of America's visionary leaders, who want to build better, stronger relationships with Latin Americans, the fastest growing segment of the American workforce.

Learning Spanish is going to open many doors for you, and it will affect you in ways that you can't even imagine. By learning Spanish, you will be able to work more efficiently and safely in almost every workplace in the nation. In addition, you will also be able to give better customer service by building stronger relationships with new Hispanic customers. And-there's another added benefit. You will raise your communication skills to a whole new level.

As an adult, learning a new language requires a certain mind-set. It takes time, patience, and more than a little stubbornness. Just think about it. You didn't learn English overnight- so you can't expect to know everything about Spanish by studying only a few weeks. Adults learn languages quite differently than children do, but you will still make progress quickly by learning practical words and phrases first.

The secret to learning Spanish is having ***self-confidence and a great sense of humor***. To build self-confidence, you must first realize that the entire learning experience is painless and fun. Naturally, you are going to make mistakes. All of us make mistakes in English! So get ready to laugh, learn, and go on from there.

If you took Spanish or another language in high school or college, you are going to be pleasantly surprised when words and phrases you thought you had forgotten begin to come back to you. That previous experience with other languages is still in your mind. It's just hidden away in a little-used filing cabinet. Soon that cabinet will open up again and that's going to help you learn new words even faster.

But there's another idea you should consider, too. What they told you in the traditional foreign language classroom was not exactly correct. There's no such thing as "***perfect Spanish***," just as there is no "***perfect English***." This leaves the door for good communication wide open!

Español is one of the world's most beautiful and expressive languages. Consider these other important facts as you begin:

- ✓ English and Spanish share a common Latin heritage, so literally thousands of words in our two languages are either ***similar*** or ***identical***.
- ✓ Your ability to communicate is the most important thing, so your grammar and pronunciation don't have to be "***perfect***" for you to be understood.
- ✓ Some very practical and common expressions in Spanish can be communicated with a few simple words.
- ✓ As the number of Latinos in the United States increases, so do your opportunities to practice. Trying to say even a phrase or two in Spanish every day will help you learn faster.
- ✓ Relax! People who enjoy their learning experiences seem to acquire Spanish at a much faster pace than others.
- ✓ Set realistic goals and establish reasonable practice habits.
- ✓ When you speak even a little Spanish, you are showing a tremendous respect for Hispanic culture and people.
- ✓ Even a little Spanish or ***poco español*** goes a long way!

As you begin the process of learning Spanish, you are going to notice a few important differences. Speaking Spanish might feel and sound a little funny to you at first. Don't worry. This is a completely normal. It's because you are using muscles in your face that English doesn't require. Also, your inner ear is accustomed to hearing you speak English. People tell me it sounds and feels like Daffy Duck is inside your head! Just keep going! With practice and perseverance speaking and understanding Spanish will begin to feel more natural to you.

Many Americans know more Spanish than they realize- and pronounce it perfectly. Look at the list on page four and see how many Spanish words you recognize already. Taking the Spanish sounds you already know and practicing them will enable you to learn new principals of the Spanish language easier and faster. This is a great way to build your confidence.

Amigos Similares y Familiares

Americano	Amigo	Hospital	Español	Doctor
Loco	Hotel	Oficina	Agua	Fiesta
Dinero	Señor	Señorita	Señora	Sombrero
Burrito	Taco	Olé	No problema	Accidente
Nachos	Salsa	Teléfono	Quesadilla	Margarita
Tequila	Tortilla	Bueno	Grande	Mucho
Blanco	Adiós	Gracias	Feliz Navidad	Hasta la vista.
Por favor	Pronto	Sí	Aplicación	Cinco de mayo

The Sounds of Spanish

No se preocupe. One of your biggest concerns about acquiring a new language will be speaking well enough so that others can understand you. *Don't worry!* Spanish is close enough to English that making a few mistakes along the way won't hurt your ability to communicate.

Here are the *five* vowel sounds in Spanish. These are the most important sounds in this language. Each vowel is pronounced the way it is written. Spanish vowels are never *silent*. Even if there are two vowels together in a word, both of them will stand up and be heard.

A   (ah)   as in mama

E   (eh)   as in "hay or the "eh" in set

I   (ee)   as in deep

O   (oh)   as in open

U   (oo)   as in spoon

Here are other sounds you'll need to remember. Always pronounce them the same way. Spanish is a very consistent language. The sounds the letters make don't shift around as they do in English.

	Spanish Letter	*English Sound*
C	(before an e or i)	s as in Sam: **cero: SAY**-row
G	(before an e or i)	h as in he: **energía**: n-air-**HE**-ah
H		silent: **hacienda**: ah-see-**N**-da
J		h as in hot: **Julio, HOO**-lee-oh
LL		y as in yoyo: **tortilla**, tor-**TEE**-ya
Ñ		ny as in canyon: **español**, es-pan-**NYOL**
QU		k as in kit: **tequila**, tay-**KEY**-la
RR		The "trilled" r sound: **burro, BOO**-row
V		v as in Victor: **Victor**, Vic-**TOR**
Z		s as in son: **Gonzales**, gone-**SA**-les

The Other Consonants - The remaining letters in Spanish are very similar to their equivalents in English.

The Spanish Alphabet
El alphabeto español

A	ah	J	HO-ta	R	AIR-ray
B	bay	K	ka	RR	EH-rray
C	say	L	L-ay	S	S-ay
CH	chay	LL	A-yea	T	tay
D	day	M	M-ay	U	oo
E	A or EH	N	N-ay	V	vay
F	f-ay	Ñ	N-yea	W	DOE-blay-vay
G	hay	O	oh	X	'a-kees
H	AH-chay	P	pay	Y	ee-gree-A-gah
I	ee	Q	coo	Z	SAY-ta

The Spanish Accent

In Spanish you will see two accent marks. Both are very important and do different things. One of the diacritical marks you will notice is called a "tilde." It is only found over the letter "N." But, don't get the Ñ confused with N. The accent mark over Ñ makes it into a different letter entirely. In fact, it's one of four letters in the Spanish alphabet that the English alphabet doesn't have. The Ñ changes the sound of the letter to a combination of "ny." You'll hear the sound that this important letter makes in the English words "canyon" and "onion."

Occasionally you will see another accent mark over a letter in a Spanish word. The accent mark or "slash" mark shows you where to place vocal emphasis. So, when you see an accent mark over a letter in a Spanish word, just say that part of the word louder. For example: José (ho-**SAY**). These accented syllables are indicated in our pronunciation guides with bold, capital letters.

Pronouncing Spanish Words

The pronunciation of Spanish words follows more regular rules than most other languages. That makes it easier to learn. Here are some tips to remember.

1. Most Spanish words that end with vowels are stressed or emphasized on the *next to the last* syllable.
2. Look for an accent mark. If the Spanish word has an accent in it, that's the emphasized syllable.
3. Words that end in consonants are stressed on the *final* syllable.

Spanish Punctuation Marks

You will see two different punctuation marks in Spanish. First there's the upside down question mark (¿). You will see it at the beginning of all questions. It's there to simply let you know that what follows is a question and you will need to give your voice an upward inflection. It's the same inflection we use in English. Then, there's the upside down exclamation mark (¡). It's there to let you know that what follows should be vocally emphasized.

Spanglish

In 1848 the treaty that ended the US-Mexican War signed over much of the Southwest to the United States. This transformed Spanish-speaking Mexicans into Americans overnight! Imagine waking up one morning and finding out you are a citizen of another country. As a result of the treaty, a new language was born that mixes the best of both worlds. Spanglish is a mixture of both our languages. Now, people who use Spanglish span generations, classes and nationalities. It's heard in pop music, seen in print, and used in conversations all through the Americas. Immigrants learning English may turn to Spanglish out of necessity and bilingual speakers use it because it's convenient. Even thought it's still frowned upon in most traditional language classes, it really is a great tool. Listed below are some of our favoritos.

Truck/Trocka	Lunch/Lonche	No parking/No parque
Yard/Yarda	Break/Breaka	Cell Phone/El cel

Some English words used as Spanglish are pronounced exactly as they are in English.

El bar	El internet
El break time	La party
El supermarket	La pizza
El email	El record
La dishwasher	El rock-n-roll
El stress	El six-pack

More Amigos Similares y Familiares

Using what you've learned about the sounds of Spanish, practice with the words listed below. Many of the words will be ones you already know or have heard, while others will be new to you. Examine the new words. Some of them will be useful to you at work. Begin by pronouncing each word on the list carefully. After you've pronounced each word, go back through the list again marking the words you can use on the job. Practice these words often to help you remember the basic sounds of español.

Easy Amigos

Matemática	Estudiante	Baño
Educación	Rosbif	Examen
Fruta	Melón	Diagrama
Clase	Temperatura	Mesa
Café	Restaurante	Corredor
Fotografía	Supervisor	Compañía
Carro	Problema	Curso
Teléfono	Sujeto	Familia
Fiesta	Música	Hamburguesa
Banco	Doctor	Hospital
Arte	Cafetería	Hotel
Jalapeño	Instrucción	Identificación
Laboratorio	Metro	Inglés
Farmacia	Museo	Parque
Servicio	Calendario	Piña
Vacación	Rápido	Pronto
Auditorio	Leche	Queso
Pera	Brócoli	Computadora
Agua	Calculadora	Vapor
Patio	Oficina	Vestíbulo
Chocolate	Panqueques	Vinagre
Limonada	Biblioteca	Vino

Muchos Ways to Practicar

The more you listen to and use your *español* the easier it will be to learn it. There are lots of great ways to practice that won't cost your any money. Try these practice techniques for improving your skills:

- ✓ Next time you're at a Mexican restaurant, order your food in *español*.
- ✓ Start slowly. Practice one sound each week.
- ✓ Read Spanish language newspapers. They are usually free and easily available.
- ✓ Listen to Spanish language radio stations.
- ✓ Watch Spanish language television via satellite.
- ✓ Rent Spanish language videos, especially cartoons.
- ✓ Buy Spanish tapes and listen to them in the car while you commute.
- ✓ And speaking of tapes, there is such a variety of Latin *música* available, something will be right for you. Listening to music is a great way to train your ears to Spanish and have fun doing it. Personally, I like anything by Carlos Santana or the Salsa of Marc Anthony. What do you like?
- ✓ Visit Internet sites like *http://www.about.com*, where you can find all kinds of information about the Spanish language. They have a wonderful newsletter that comes to you free via e-mail. Most search engines, like Yahoo, have some sort of Spanish section.
- ✓ Next time you listen to a baseball game, keep track of all the Hispanic names you hear.
- ✓ Practice your Spanish every time the opportunity presents itself. This is the only way to get over your nervousness.
- ✓ Try to learn with a friend at work and practice together.

What practice habits work for you?
Share them with us at:
info@speakeasyspanish.com

SpeakEasy's Tips and Techniques for Comunicación

Remember, when you're trying to communicate with a person who is "limited in English proficiency," *patience is a virtue*! Here are some easy things you can do to make the conversation easier for both of you. For more information on LEP visit this web site: www.lep.gov

✓ Speak slowly and distinctly.

✓ Do not use slang expressions or colorful terms.

✓ Get straight to the point! Unnecessary words cloud your meaning.

✓ Speak in a normal tone. Speaking *loudly* doesn't help anyone understand you any better!

✓ Look for cues to meaning in body language and facial expressions. Use gestures of your own to get your point across.

✓ You may not receive good eye contact.

✓ Latinos tend to stand closer to each other than North Americans do when they talk to each other, so your personal space could feel crowded. Stand your ground!

✓ Feel free to use gestures and body language of your own to communicate.

✓ Because of the way languages are learned, it is likely that the person you are talking to understands more of what you are saying, than he is able to verbalize. *So, be careful what you say!* No matter what the language, we always understand the bad words first!

Tips & Tidbits

Throughout your book look for the light bulb you see above. This section will give you helpful hints and cultural information that will help you learn easily.

Beginning Words & Phrases

Well, let's get started! In no time you will start gaining confidence. Latinos will be delighted that you are trying to speak *español*. Even if you can't remember a whole phrase, use the words you know. Thank you *gracias* and please *por favor* go a long way toward establishing a rapport.

How many of these common words and phrases do you know?

English	Español	Guide
Hi!	¡Hola!	**OH**-la
How are you?	¿Cómo está?	**KO**-mo ace-**TA**
Fine	Muy bien.	mooy b-**N**
So so	Así así	ah-**SEE** ah-**SEE**
Bad	Mal	mal
Good morning	Buenos días	boo-**WAY**-nos **DEE**-ahs
Good afternoon	Buenas tardes	boo-**WAY**-nas TAR-days
Good night	Buenas noches.	boo-**WAY**-nas **NO**-chase
Sir or Mister	Señor	sen-**YOUR**
Mrs. or Ma'am	Señora	sen-**YOUR**-ah
Miss	Señorita	sen-your- **REE**-ta
What's your name?	¿Cómo se llama?	**KO**-mo say **YA**-ma
My name is ___.	Me llamo ___.	may **YA**-mo
Nice to meet you.	¡Mucho gusto!	**MOO**-cho **GOO**-stow
Thank you.	Gracias.	**GRA**-see-ahs
Please!	¡Por favor!	pour-fa-**VOR**
You're welcome. The pleasure is mine.	De nada. El gusto es mío.	day **NA** da el **GOO**-stow es **ME**-oh
I'm sorry.	Lo siento.	low-see-**N**-toe
Excuse me.	¡Perdón!	pear-**DON**
Bless you!	¡Salud!	sah-**LEWD**
We'll see you!	¡Hasta la vista	**AH**-sta la **VEE**-sta
Good-bye	Adiós	ah-dee-**OS**

Spanish Sounds Rápido – What Do I Do Now?

Be honest! One of the reasons you are hesitant to speak Spanish is that it sounds so fast! Naturally, you're afraid you won't understand. Here are some phrases that will help you. Make learning them a priority. *¿Comprende, amigo?*

English	Español	Guide
I don't understand.	No comprendo.	no com-**PREN**-doe
Do you understand	¿Comprende?	com-**PREN**-day
I speak a little Spanish.	Hablo poco español.	**AH**-blow **POE**-co es-pan-**NYOL**
Do you speak English?	¿Habla inglés?	**AH**-bla eng-**LACE**
Repeat, please.	Repita, por favor.	ray-**PETE**-ah pour fa-**VOR**
I'm studying Spanish.	Estudio español.	es-**TOO**-dee-oh es-pan-**NYOL**
Write it, please	Escribe, por favor	es-**SCRE**-bay pour fa-**VOR**
Speak more slowly, please.	Habla más despacio, por favor.	**AH**-bla mas des-**PA**-see-oh pour fa-**VOR**
Thanks for your patience.	Gracias por su paciencia.	**GRA**-see-ahs pour sue pa-see-**N**-see-ah
How do you say it in Spanish?	¿Como se dice en español?	**CO**-mo say **DEE**-say n ace-pan-**NYOL**
Where are you from?	¿De dónde es?	day **DON**-day ace
May I help you?	¿Puedo servirle?	pooh-**A**-doe seer-**VEER**-lay

The key here is <u>not</u> to pánico.

Your Spanish-speaking employee or friend is having just as much trouble understanding you, as you are having understanding them! Hang in there! Between the two of you, *comunicación* will begin to take place.

SpeakEasy's Conversaciones

Practice Conversation I

USTED: Good morning, Sir.

SR.GARCÍA   Good morning. How are you?

USTED   Fine, thanks. How are you?

SR. GARCÍA   OK, thanks.

Practice Conversation II

USTED   May I help you? My name is _____.
I speak a little Spanish. What's your name?

SRA. GARCÍA: My name is Carla García
                Hernandez. I speak a
                little English.

USTED   Nice to meet you.

SRA. GARCÍA   Yes, nice to meet you.

¡Hola!

Can you say the following?

✓ Good morning or hi

✓ My name is _____.

✓ I speak a little Spanish.

✓ Do you speak English?

✓ Slower, please. Thank you.

¿Cuál Es Su Nombre Completo?
What Is Your Complete Name?

Hispanic Names Have Four Parts

First Name	Middle Name	Father's Surname	Mother's Surname
Primer Nombre	Segundo Nombre	Apellido Paterno	Apellido Materno
Carlos	Jesús	Santana	Rodríguez
José	Pedro	Cuervo	Álvarez
Poncho	Luis	Villa	García
Carmen	Elena	Miranda	Rivera

Start with: Señor, Señora, or Señorita

Use Both Names Or Only The Father's Last Name

Sr. Santana   Sr. Cuervo
Sr. Villa   Sra. Miranda

When A Woman Marries

She Keeps Her Father's Apellido Paterno
She Drops Her Apellido Materno
Last Is Her Husband's Apellido Paterno
Ask for her "Apellido Paterno de Esposo"

Children Have The Apellido Paterno of Both Father and Mother

*If Carlos Santana married Carmen Miranda,
what is the Nombre Completo of the bebé*

José Carlos ???? ?????

Answer: José Carlos Santana Miranda

Spanish Nouns

Can words *really* have a gender?

¡Sí! Spanish belongs to the "romance" language family. It doesn't have anything to do with love, but it has a lot to do with the Romans. In ancient times people had the same trouble learning languages that they do today—except that there were no cassette tapes, CDs, PDAs or very many foreign language teachers. In those days, there weren't many schools for that matter! Consequently, most folks were on their own when it came to learning another language.

To help the difficult process along, words were placed into categories based on how they sounded. This organized the material and made it easier to learn. Old-world languages had many different categories and because the categories were often called "masculine," "feminine," or even "neuter," people began talking about words in terms of their gender. Even though the word "gender" is misleading, the tendency to group words by sound helped people learn new languages more quickly.

Because Spanish evolved from Latin, it has maintained two category divisions for thousands of years. The categories are called masculine and feminine. Even though Spanish can and will evolve, the concept of categories in español is not likely to change.

Here are the most important points to remember about nouns and their categories:

NOUN A person, place or thing

1. Usually, the words are grouped by how they sound, not by what they mean. There will always be a few exceptions!

2. Languages are a lot like the people who use them: They don't always follow the rules!

3. If the Spanish noun is referring to a person, the letter will often indicate the sex of that individual. For example: a doctor, who is a man is a "doctor," while a woman, who is a doctor is a "doctora."

4. Words in the "masculine" category usually end with the letter "O".

5. Words in the "feminine" category usually end with the letter "A".

6. El, la, los and las are very important words. They all mean "the". They are the clues you need to tell you a word's category.

El (masculine category – singular)   El niño, El muchacho
Los (masculine category – plural)   Los niños, Los muchachos
La (feminine category – singular)   La niña, La muchacha
Las (feminine category – plural)   Las niñas, Las muchachas

A Word about Adjectives

In Spanish, most common, descriptive words or adjectives come after the nouns they describe. Conversationally, this is going to require some practice. While you are learning, don't be too concerned about misplacing an adjective or failing to change its final letter to match the noun's category. These are the kinds of common mistakes that everyone makes— even native speakers.

Where the position of adjectives is concerned, there are some notable exceptions. Numbers and other adjectives which show quantity usually come before the noun they describe. That's the way we do it in English!

Descriptive words match the noun by both category and number.

La casa bonita or las casas bonitas

Tips & Tidbits

Always remember that learning the word is the most important thing, not which category it is! When you are trying to say something, small words like "el" or "la" only mean the. They don't give any clues to what you are trying to say to the person that you are speaking with. Learning the fine points of grammar can wait until you are a master of survival Spanish. First, concentrate on learning the words you need to know!

ADJECTIVE Describes a noun

The Essentials of Spanish Verbs

There are basically three types of regular verbs in Spanish. The last two letters on the end of the verb determines how it is to be treated.

Listed below are the three most common types of regular verb endings.

- ✓ AR - Hablar – to speak
- ✓ ER - Comprender – to understand
- ✓ IR - Vivir – to live

In Survival Spanish, we are going to focus on talking about ourselves and talking to another person. That's the most common type of "one on one" communication.

When you want to say I speak, I understand, or I live, change the last two letters of the verb to an "O".

- ✓ Hablo
- ✓ Comprendo
- ✓ Vivo

When asking a question, such as do you speak, do you understand, or do you live, change the ending to an "A" or an "E". The change in letter indicates that you are speaking to someone else.

- ✓ Habla
- ✓ Comprende
- ✓ Vive

To make a sentence negative, simply put "no" in front of the verb.

- ✓ No hablo
- ✓ No comprendo
- ✓ No vivo

VERB Shows action or state of being

¡Acción!

There are so many English friendly *acción* words in the Spanish "AR" verb family. Many of them bear a strong resemblance to English verbs- and most of them share a simple, regular nature. They are a very important asset in on-the-job communication. We picked a few of our favorites to get you started. Look closely at the list on page 19. On it you will recognize many comforting similarities between our languages that are practical too! Changing one letter will really expand your conversational skills.

In on-the-job conversations, people tend to use "I" and "you" to start many sentences. Of all the pronouns, these two are the most powerful and will work the hardest for you. So, that's where we'll start.

Here's an important difference between our languages. In English, the use of pronouns is essential because most of our verbs end the same way. For example, with I speak and you speak; speak remains the same. Our pronouns make all the difference. This isn't true in Spanish. Spanish-speaking people are listening for the letter on the end of the verb. That's what indicates who or what is being talked about. In most cases, you might not hear a pronoun. That's another reason that Spanish might sound a little fast to you: A whole series of words that are important in English are routinely eliminated in Spanish!

Try this: Treat the verbs in the "AR" family as you would "to speak" or "hablar." End the verb with an "o" when you're talking about yourself; "hablo" or "I speak". Change the verb ending from an "o" to an "a" for "habla" or "you speak." Use this form when you're talking to someone else.

English	Español	Guide
I need	Necesito	nay-say-SEE-toe
You need	Necesita	nay-say-SEE-ta

**Note: To make a sentence negative, say no in front of the verb. No necesito. No necesita.

The Sweet 16 Verbs

English	Español	Guide
1. To ask	Preguntar	prey-goon-**TAR**
2. To bother	Molestar	mo-les-**TAR**
3. To call	Llamar	ya-**MAR**
4. To carry	Llevar	yea-**VAR**
5. To cooperate	Cooperar	co-op-air-**RAR**
6. To forget	Olvidar	ohl-v-**DAR**
7. To look at	Mirar	mear-**RAHER**
8. To need	Necesitar	nay-say-see-**TAR**
9. To observe	Observar	ob-ser-**VAR**
10. To pay	Pagar	pa-**GAR**
11. To prepare	Preparar	pray-pa-**RAR**
12. To return	Regresar	ray-grey-**SAR**
13. To study	Estudiar	es-too-d-**ARE**
14. To use	Usar	oo-**SAR**
15. To teach	Enseñar	n-sen-**YAR**
16. To work	Trabajar	tra-baa-**HAR**

**The "Sweet 16 Verbs" were suggested by participants in SpeakEasy Spanish programs.

Which verbs in the Sweet 16 do you use most often? List your top six:

1. _____

2. _____

3. _____

4. _____

5. _____

6. _____

Now take your top six, change the AR ending to an "a" and make a negative sentence by adding no at the beginning. For example: No necesita. You don't need.

1. _____

2. _____

3. _____

4. _____

5. _____

6. _____

> **Tú and Usted**
>
> In español there are two words for "you": Usted and tú.
>
> Usted is for adults, strangers and acquaintances.
> Tú is for children and close friends.
>
> When using usted, your verb will end in the letter "a."
>
> When using tú, your verb should end with "as."

Which verbs would you like to see on the list? Write them below:

1. _____

2. _____

3. _____

4. _____

5. _____

6. _____

Tips & Tidbits

On your journey to Spanish proficiency, make prioritizing your vocabulary your *número uno prioridad*! Go through the "sweet 16" verb list in the table above with different colors of markers. Highlight your "A" list in your favorite color. Look at the vocabulary that remains. Go through it again with a different color- one you don't like so much, and make it your "B" list. Don't begin on your "B" list until you are comfortable with your first choices.

Para Practicar

Use verbs from the Sweet 16 to say the following. Use "usted" for one set and tú for another. Change the end of the verb from "a" to "as" as needed.

1. You teach _____

2. Don't use _____

3. Prepare _____

4. I need *(Remember: Pronouns are often eliminated in Spanish)*

   _____

5. I work _____

6. To inform_____

7. Don't bother _____

8. You observe _____

9. Ask _____

10. Cooperate, please _____

¡Necesito una breaka!

21

The Big Five - Los Cinco Grandes

Now that you have had the opportunity to learn about the tremendous number of verbs that follow regular patterns in Spanish, it's time to take a look at others that don't follow the rules. They are unpredictable, but they are very important. In fact, they reflect some of man's oldest concepts. That's why they tend to be irregular. These words were in use long before language rules and patterns were set. So, here they are: to be (2), to have, to make, and to go. Because they don't follow the rules, you will need to memorize them, but that should be easy because you will use and hear them often.

In Spanish there are two verbs that mean *"to be"*. In English, that's I am, you are, he is, etc. The Spanish version is **ser** and **estar**. **Ser** is used to express permanent things like your nationality or profession. **Estar** is used when talking about location or conditions that change like a person's health.

Ser

Yo **soy**	Nosotros **somos**
Tú **eres**	
Él **es**	Ellos **son**
Ella **es**	Ellas **son**
Usted **es**	Ustedes **son**

Estar

Yo **estoy**	Nosotros **estamos**
Tú **estás**	
Él **está**	Ellos **están**
Ella **está**	Ellas **están**
Usted **está**	Ustedes **están**

The verb *"to have"* in Spanish is *muy importante*. In English we say that we are hot, cold, hungry, thirsty, right, wrong or sleepy, but in Spanish those are conditions that you have. Some of those expressions mean something totally different than you expected if you get the verbs confused, so be careful!

Tener

Yo **tengo**	Nosotros **tenemos**
Tú **tienes**	
Él **tiene**	Ellos **tienen**
Ella **tiene**	Ellas **tienen**
Usted **tiene**	Ustedes **tienen**

In Spanish the verb that means, *"to do"* also means, *"to make."* It's not unusual for one verb to have multiple meanings. There are many expressions that require the use of this verb, but you will use it most when you talk about the weather. That's a safe subject and one that everyone, the world over, discusses! **¿Qué tiempo hace?** What's the weather? **Hace frío.** (It's cold.) **Hace sol.** (It's sunny). **Hace calor.** (It's hot) **Hace viento** (It's windy.). Here's two exceptions: **Está lloviendo.** (It's raining.) and **Está nevando.** (It's snowing.)

Hacer

Yo **hago**	Nosotros **hacemos**
Tú **haces**	
Él **hace**	Ellos **hacen**
Ella **hace**	Ellas **hacen**
Usted **hace**	Ustedes **hacen**.

The last of the big five is perhaps the easiest to use. It's the verb that means, *"to go"*. In Spanish, that's **ir**. It's pronounced like the English word ear. Both in English and in Spanish, we use parts of it to make the future tense, in other words, to talk about things that we are going to do. Look at the parts of ir. Then look back at the parts of the verb ser. Do you notice any similarities?

Ir

Yo **voy**	Nosotros **vamos**
Tú **vas**	
Él **va**	Ellos **van**
Ella **va**	Ellas **van**
Usted **va**	Ustedes **van**

When you want to say something that you are going to do, start with I'm going or voy. Next, insert the word "a" and the basic verb that states what it is that you're going to do. Try it! It's easy. Here are some examples.

Voy a visitar a mi familia.	I am going to visit my family.
Voy a organizar los trabajadores.	I am going to organize the workers.
Mario va a comprar las plantas.	Mario is going to buy the plants.

**The whole concept of irregular verbs is can be quite daunting. Don't let it defeat you! We have many verbs like this in English. In fact, every language has them. The only way to master them is to practice by using them. Make them your own! Try writing different parts of a verb on your desk calendar. That way, it will be there in front of you every time you look down. When you see it, say it to yourself. Then, you'll have it conquered in no time.

Para Practicar

Using what you've learned in the preceding chapters, write these phrases in español.

1. I am going to work. _____

2. I am going to finish._____

3. Where is Ramón? _____

4. Where is Carlos? _____

5. I am Tim. _____

6. He is Alan. _____

7. She is Amy. _____

8. I have five sisters. _____

9. He has three brothers. _____

10. Juan has four children. _____

How do you feel? - ¿Cómo te sientes?

In the summertime it can get really hot. Suppose you are visiting in a Latino student's home and to express your discomfort in Spanish you say: "Estoy calor." Your host, a very polite, diplomatic person, looks at you and has to refrain from laughing. Why? In English we use adjectives to describe how we are feeling. So, you think you've said, I am hot," which doesn't mean that you are sick and have a fever. To say, "I am hot," would literally mean to your Spanish host that you are hot to the touch of a hand. Of course this sounds strange and silly to us, but *"Tengo calor"* is the expression you need. *Remember that our English idioms often sound very strange to others.*

As a rule the verb **tener** is used to describe physical conditions, whereas in English we use the verb *to be.*

Español	**English**
Tener calor	To be hot
Tener hambre	To be hungry
Tener frío.	To be cold
Tener vergüenza	To be ashamed
Tener dolor	To be in pain.
Tener miedo de	To be afraid of
Tener razón	To be right
Tener sed	To be thirsty
Tener sueño	To be sleepy
Tener *xx* años	To be *xx* years old

Para Practicar:
Work with an amigo. Using tengo, I have, and tiene, you have, ask the following questions. Remember to start with no if you want to make your statement negative.

1. Are you hungry?_____

2. Are you thirsty? _____

3. Are you hot? _____

4. Are you cold? _____

5. How old are you? _____

6. Are you afraid of the doctor? _____

7. Are you in pain? _____

8. I am ashamed. _____

9. I'm not hungry _____

What's the Weather? - ¿Qué tiempo hace?

No matter what the culture is, a general topic for discussion is always the weather. Discussing the weather in Spanish requires a different verb from the one used in English. So, if you said to your host, "Está frío," he or she would think that you were talking about something you had touched. In Spanish use the verb **hacer** (to do or to make) to describe the weather. It's one of the big five irregulars

Español	English
Hace buen tiempo	To be nice weather
Hace calor	To be hot
Hace fresco	To be cool
Hace sol	To be sunny
Hace viento	To be windy
Hace frío	To be cold
Lluvia	Rain
Llover	To rain.
¿Qué tiempo hace?	What's the weather?

Tips & Tidbits
In America we use the Fahrenheit scale for measuring the temperature. Latin Americans use the Celsius scale. What is the difference?

Special Uses of Ser and Estar

The verbs **ser** and **estar** both mean the same thing in English: ***to be***. In both languages it is a very irregular verb. (I am, he/she/it is, we are, they are).

Ser is used for permanent qualities or characteristics.
Soy de Carolina del Norte. I'm from North Carolina.

Estar is used to express temporary conditions and locations.
¿Dónde está Carolina del Norte? Where is North Carolina?

USES OF SER

A. To express an inherent quality or characteristic of a subject.
    La puerta es de madera.   The door is made of wood.

B.   **La escuela es enorme.**   The school is enormous.
    Las maestras son importantes.   Teachers are important.

C. To describe or identify the subject.
    Mi amigo es médico.   My friend is a doctor.
    El estudiante es alto.   The student is tall.
    Nuestros doctores son intelligentes.   Our doctors are smart.

D. To say where something or someone is from.
    El visitante es cubano.   The visitor is cuban.
    Ellas son mexicanas.   They are Mexican.
    La historia es de Argentina.   The story is from Argentina.

E. To express ownership.
    Este es mi auto.   This is my car.
    Este es mi libro.   This is my book.

F. To express time and dates.
    ¿Qué hora es?   What time is it?
    Hoy es el nueve de junio.   Today is the 9th of June.

G. With impersonal expressions.
    Es importante estudiar.   It's important to study.
    Es necesario leer.   It's necessary read.

USES OF ESTAR

A. To express location or position.
    Estoy en la oficina.   I am in the office.
    Charlotte está en Carolina del Norte.   Charlotte is in North Carolina.
    La biblioteca está en el cuarto piso.   The library is on the 4th floor.

B. To indicate the state or temporary condition of the subject.
    El estudiante está enfermo.   The student is sick.
    Su madre está bien.   Your mother is well.
    El café está caliente.   The coffee is hot.
    ¿Cómo está usted?   How are you?

Fill in the blank with the correct form of ser.
1. El Dr. Martinez _____ un hombre grande.
2. Las escuelas _____ importantes.
3. La biblioteca _____ moderno.
4. Nuestros _____ visitantes.
5. Yo _____ maestra.

Fill in the blank with the correct form of estar.
1. El estudiante _____ bien.
2. Ellos _____ enfermos.
3. María _____ cansada. (tired)
4. La sopa _____ fría. (cold)
5. Yo _____ en el baño.

Fill in the blank with the correct form of ser or estar according to the meaning expressed in the sentence.
1. Charlotte _____ en el centro del Carolina del Norte.
2. Carlos _____ director.
3. ¿Cómo _____ usted?
4. Yo _____ la consejera.
5. Raleigh _____ la capital del estado.
6. ¿Dónde _____ los estudiantes.
7. El asistente _____ cubano.
8. ¿Qué hora _____?
9. Mi oficina _____ en la universidad.
10. _____ Julie.

Descriptions or Descripciones

Describing things in Spanish can present problems for English speakers. There are three reasons why this gives us trouble. First, there is the location of the adjective. In English, descriptive words go in front of the noun like white cat, for example. In Spanish, the noun is the most important element, so it comes first (*gato blanco*). However, it gets a little more complicated because there are a few adjectives that are placed before the noun- and they are very common: For example: large or *grande* (*grande gato blanco*). Next, since Spanish nouns are divided into masculine and feminine categories, the descriptive word should match it by category and by number (singular or plural). This leads us to challenge number three: changing the spelling of the adjective. You might need to change a final "o" to an "a" to change the category. Here is a list of descriptive words that can be used in almost any profession.

English	Español	English	Español
Alive	Vivo	**Dead**	Muerto
Good	Bueno	**Bad**	Malo
Better	Mejor	**Worse**	Peor
Big	Grande	**Small**	Pequeño
Clean	Limpio	**Dirty**	Sucio
Hot	Caliente	**Cold**	Frío
Sane	Cuerdo	**Crazy**	Loco
Safe	Seguro	**Dangerous**	Peligroso
Easy	Fácil	**Difficult**	Difícil
Full	Lleno	**Empty**	Vacío
Fast	Rápido	**Slow**	Lento
Hard	Duro	**Soft**	Blando
New	Nuevo	**Old**	Viejo
Rich	Rico	**Poor**	Pobre
Pretty	Bonito	**Ugly**	Feo
Quiet	Tranquilo	**Restless**	Inquieto
Tall	Alto	**Short**	Bajo
Well	Bien	**Sick**	Enfermo
Strong	Fuerte	**Weak**	Débil

Los Números How Much - ¿Cuánto?

Number	Español	Pronunciation Guide
0	Cero	**SAY**-row
1	Uno	**OO**-no
2	Dos	dose
3	Tres	trays
4	Cuatro	coo-**AH**-trow
5	Cinco	**SINK**-oh
6	Seis	**SAY**-ees
7	Siete	see-**A**-tay
8	Ocho	**OH**-cho
9	Nueve	new-**A**-Vay
10	Diez	dee-**ACE**
11	Once	**ON**-say
12	Doce	**DOSE**-a
13	Trece	**TRAY**-say
14	Catorce	ca-**TOR**-say
15	Quince	**KEEN**-say
16	Diez y seis	dee-**ACE**-e-**SAY**-ees
17	Diez y siete	dee-**ACE**-e-see-**ATE**-tay
18	Diez y ocho	dee-**ACE**-e-**OH**-cho
19	Diez y nueve	dee-**ACE**-e-new-**A**-vay
20	Veinte	**VAIN**-tay
21	Veinte y uno	**VAIN**-tay -e-**OO**-no
22	Veinte y dos	**VAIN**-tay -e- dose
23	Veinte y tres	**VAIN**-tay -e- trays
24	Veinte y cuatro	**VAIN**-tay -e- Coo-**AH**-trow
25	Veinte y cinco	**VAIN**-tay -e- **SINK**-oh
26	Veinte y seis	**VAIN**-tay -e-**SAY**-ees
27	Veinte y siete	**VAIN**-tay -e- see-**A**-tay
28	Veinte y ocho	**VAIN**-tay -e **OH**-cho -
29	Veinte y nueve	**VAIN**-tay -e- new-**A**-vay
30	Treinta	**TRAIN**-ta
40	Cuarenta	kwah-**RAIN**-ta
50	Cincuenta	seen-**KWAIN**-ta
60	Sesenta	say-**SAIN**-ta
70	Setenta	say-**TAIN**-ta
80	Ochenta	oh-**CHAIN**-ta
90	Noventa	no-**VAIN**-ta
100	Cien	see-**IN**
200	Doscientos	dose-see-**N**-toes
300	Trescientos	tray-see-**N**-toes
400	Cuatrocientos	coo-**AH**-troh-see-**N**-toes
500	Quinientos	keen-e-**N**-toes
600	Seiscientos	**SAY**-ees-see- **N**-toes
700	Setecientos	**SAY**-tay-see- **N**-toes
800	Ochocientos	**OH**-choh- see- **N**-toes
900	Novecientos	**NO**-Vay-see- **N**-toes
1,000	Mil	meal

Los Días de la Semana y los Meses del Año
Los Días de la Semana

English	Español	Guide
Monday	lunes	**LOON**-ace
Tuesday	martes	**MAR**-tays
Wednesday	miércoles	me-**AIR**-co-lace
Thursday	jueves	who-**WAVE**-ace
Friday	viernes	vee-**AIR**-nace
Saturday	sábado	**SAH**-ba-doe
Sunday	domingo	doe-**MING**-go

It's important to remember when expressing a date in Spanish give the number of the day first followed by the month. Use this format:
El (date) de (month).

Los Meses del Año

English	Español	Guide
January	enero	n-**NAY**-row
February	febrero	fay-**BRAY**-row
March	marzo	**MAR**-so
April	abril	ah-**BRILL**
May	mayo	**MY**-oh
June	junio	**WHO**-knee-oh
July	julio	**WHO**-lee-oh
August	agosto	ah-**GOSE**-toe
September	septiembre	sep-tee-**EM**-bray
October	octubre	oc-**TOO**-bray
November	noviembre	no-vee-**EM**-bray
December	diciembre	dee-see-**EM**-bray

Your job starts (*day of the week*) el (*number*) de (*month*).
Su empleo comienza lunes, el 11 de octubre.

Your appointment is Monday the 5th of May.
Su cita es lunes el cinco de mayo.

Practicing Numbers & Dates

Practice these important items by using numbers, days of the week, and months of the year:

✓ Your social security number

✓ Your driver's license number

✓ The numbers in your address

✓ Your zip code

✓ Your phone number

✓ Your birth date

✓ Your children's birth dates

✓ The dates of holidays

✓ License tags of the cars in front of you, when you are stopped in traffic. Combine the Spanish alphabet with this exercise.

✓ Phone numbers you see on billboards

✓ Numbers found on street signs

✓ Phone numbers when you dial them at work or at home

✓ The appointments on your personal calendar

✓ Your wedding anniversary

✓ The dates of all your Spanish classes or practice sessions

¿Qué Hora Es?
What Time Is It?

The concept of time is something that varies from culture to culture. Many countries put less emphasis on being on time than Americans do. For Latinos working in America, this is rapidly changing. They quickly learn the value of *puntualidad. Es importante!*

Learning to tell time is another good way to put your numbers in Spanish to good use . *¿Qué hora es?* means *what time is it?*

It's one o'clock.	**Es la una.**
It's two o'clock.	**Son las dos.**
It's 3:30.	**Son las tres y media.**
It's 5:45.	**Son las seis menos quince.**

Use the phrases *de la mañana* to indicate morning and *de la tarde* to indicate afternoon. Also midnight is *medianoche*. Noon is *mediodía*.

To find out at what time something takes place ask: *¿A qué hora…?*

¿A qué hora es la reunión?	**What time is the meeting?**
¿A qué hora termina?	**What time do you finish?**

Spanish speakers sometimes use the 24-hour clock for departures and arrivals of trains and flights, etc.

12.05	las doce cero cinco
17.52	las diez y siete cincuenta y dos
23.10	las veinte y tres diez
07.15	las siete quince

Para practicar

1. Using the word for meeting, la reunion, say that the meeting takes place on the hour throughout your regular workday. *La reunión es a las ocho.*
2. Tell Sr. Rojas what time your store opens and closes.
3. Using the days of the week and the time to explain a work schedule. Your work schedule is…. *Su horario es…..*

Scheduling an Appointment

Anyone from the school secretary, counselor, principal or teacher will need to schedule appointments. An appointment is called a *cita*. List the name of the individual that the appointment is with first. Then circle the day of the week and add the number for the day. Finally, circle the month and add the time. The phrase at the bottom of this form simply asks the individual to arrive ten minutes early for the appointment.

Usted tiene una cita importante con _____.

La cita es   lunes   el _____ de   enero   a las _____.

              martes   febrero

              miércoles   marzo

              jueves   abril

              viernes   mayo

                                       junio

                                     julio

                                   agosto

                                   septiembre

                                   octubre

                                   noviembre

                                   diciembre

Favor de llegar 10 minutos antes del tiempo de su cita ¡Gracias!

The Questions Everyone Should Know

English	Español	Guide
Who?	¿Quién?	key-**N**
Whose?	¿De quién?	day key-**N**
What?	¿Qué?	kay
Which?	¿Cuál?	coo-**ALL**
When?	¿Cuándo?	**KWAN**-doe
Where?	¿Dónde?	**DON**-day
Why?	¿Por qué?	pour **KAY**
How?	¿Cómo?	**CO**-mo
What's happening?	¿Qué pasa?	kay **PA**-sa
What happened?	¿Qué pasó?	kay **PA**-so
How much?	¿Cuánto?	**KWAN**-toe
How many	¿Cuántos?	**KWAN**-toes

When you ask a question in Spanish, it will take on the same form as a question does in English. Start with the question word that asks the information you need. Follow the question word with a verb, and give your voice an upward inflection.

In Spanish you can also make a question by ending your sentence with ¿no? Here's an example: Cancún está en México, ¿no? When you end a sentence with "no" like this, it takes on the meaning of "isn't it."

The Most Common Questions

How are you?   ¿Cómo está?
How much does it cost?   ¿Cuánto cuesta?
Where are you from?   ¿De dónde es?

Did you notice the upside down question mark (¿) at the beginning of each question? All questions in Spanish begin with this punctuation mark. All exclamatory phrases like, Hi! Begin with an upside down exclamation point like this: ¡Hola! You can do this on your word processor. Refer to "Typing in Spanish with Microsoft Word" in your table of contents for details.

Getting the Información
La entrevista – The Interview

Listed below are the most common questions used during an interview. It's not always necessary to make a complete sentence to have good communication. The information you are asking for is much more important than the phrase "what is your"? As long as you remember to make what you say *sound* like a question by giving your voice an *upward* inflection, people will interpret what you've said *as* a question. Use the form on the following page. Work with a partner to practice giving and receiving information. Make up new answers about yourself for each practice session. You will always be asking the same questions, but the answers you get will always be different!

What's your. . .   **¿Cuál es su. . .**
                                        Coo-ALL ace sue

English	Español
Full name	Nombre completo
First name	Primer nombre
Last name	Apellido
Paternal surname	Apellido paterno
Maternal surname	Apellido materno
Address	Dirección
Apartment number	Número de apartamento
Age	Edad
Date of birth	Fecha de nacimiento
Nationality	Nacionalidad
Place of birth	Lugar de nacimiento
Place of employment	Lugar de empleo
Occupation	Ocupación
Home telephone number	Número de teléfono de su casa
Work telephone number	Número de teléfono de su empleo
Marital status	Estado civil
Driver's license number	Número de licencia
Social security number	Número de seguro social

Información Básica
Imprima por favor

Fecha: _____
　　　　Mes　　Día　　Año

Sr.
Sra.
Srta. _____
Primer Nombre　Segundo Nombre　Apellido Paterno　Apellido Materno (Esposo)

Dirección: _____
Calle

_____
Ciudad　　　　　Estado　　　　　Zona postal

Teléfono: Casa _____　**Empleo** _____

　　　　Cel _____　**Fax** _____

Correo electrónico _____

Número de seguro social: _____ - _____ - _____

Nombre de otros niños: _____

Fecha de nacimiento _____
　　　　Mes　　Día　　Año

Número de la licencia: _____

Ocupación: _____

Lugar de empleo _____

Estado civil:　　Casado (a)
　　　　　　　　　Soltero (a)
　　　　　　　　　Divorciado (a)
　　　　　　　　　Separado (a)
　　　　　　　　　Viudo (a)

Nombre de esposo: _____
　　　Primer Nombre　Segundo Nombre　Apellido Paterno　Apellido Materno
Nombre de esposa: _____
　　Primer Nombre　Segundo Nombre　Apellido Paterno　Apellido Materno/Esposo

En caso de emergencia: _____**Teléfono:** _____

Firma: _____　　**Fecha:** _____

The Family - La Familia

Family values are extremely important to Latinos. This is something all of us have in common. Many Latinos have left their families in their native countries to come here for economic reasons. No sacrifice is too great for *la familia*.

Children are considered to be precious gifts. Wives, mothers and grandmothers are greatly respected. Remember that all Hispanics have their mother's surname or *materno apellido*. You are going to hear members of the family from your Hispanic customers. It's something all of us like to talk about!

English	Español	Guide
Aunt	Tía	**TEE**-ah
Uncle	Tío	**TEE**-oh
Brother	Hermano	air-**MAN**-oh
Sister	Hermana	air-**MAN**-ah
Brother-in-law	Cuñado	coon-**YA**-doe
Sister-in-law	Cuñada	coon-**YA**-da
Child	Niño, niña	**KNEE**-nyo, **KNEE**-nya
Cousin	Primo, prima	**PRE**-mo, **PRE**-ma
Daughter	Hija	**E**-ha
Son	Hijo	**E**-ho
Daughter-in-law	Nuera	new-**AIR**-rah
Son-in-law	Yerno	**YEAIR**-no
Father	Padre	**PA**-dray
Mother	Madre	**MA**-dray
Father-in-law	Suegro	soo-**A**-grow
Mother-in-law	Suegra	soo-**A**-gra
Granddaughter	Nieta	knee-**A**-tah
Grandson	Nieto	knee-**A**-toe
Grandfather	Abuelo	ah-boo-**A**-low
Grandmother	Abuela	ah-boo-**A**-la
Husband	Esposo	es-**PO**-so
Wife	Esposa	es-**POE**-sa

Para Practicar

Using the verb tener (to have), tell your practice partner how many relatives you have in your family. Start like this: Tengo or I have. Follow that with the number and the member of the family that you are talking about. You will find more about tener in the next chapter. Even though it isn't a regular verb, it's very practical. You will use it in many different ways.

En mi familia.....

Write the following sentences in Spanish.

1. I have two sons. _____

2. I have three daughters _____

3. He has four cousins _____

4. My wife has five cousins _____

5. My wife's name is _____

6. I have three uncles _____

7. I have six aunts _____

8. I have no brothers _____

9. I have one (una) sister _____

10. She has no children_____ _____

**In this exercise use the word "mi" for "my."*

Employee Benefits & Human Resources
Beneficios y Recoursos Humanos

Many schools are hiring Hispanic employees to fill a variety of positions. In some areas the diversity of the school staff can be as great as that of the student body. Making sure things run smoothly in a multicultural work environment can be stressful. Language and cultural barriers can become incredibly challenging. From teachers, to assistants, security personnel and others your Spanish-speaking workforce will include a variety of employees. When it's time for you to explain employment policies and benefit packages, go slowly. The concept of tax deductions, insurance benefits, retirement and Social Security can be new to some Hispanic employees.

English	Español	Guide
Benefits	Beneficios	ben-nay-**FEE**-see-ohs
Check	Cheque	**CHEC**-kay
Disability	Incapacidad	n-ka-pah-see-**DAD**
Permanent resident card	Tarjeta de residencia permanente	tar-**HEY**-ta day ray-see-**DEN**-cee-ah pear-me-**NIN**-tay
Holidays	Días festivos	**DEE**-ahs fes-**TEE**-vos
Insurance	Seguro	say-**GOO**-row
License	Licencia	lee-**SEN**-see-ah
Medical Insurance	Seguro médico	say-**GOO**-row **MAY**-dee-co
Overtime	Sobre tiempo	so-bray-tee-**M**-po
Paid vacations	Vacaciones pagadas	va-ca-see-**ON**-ace pah-**GA**-das
Paycheck	Paga	**PAH**-ga
Retirement	Retiro *or* Jubilación	ray-**TEE**-row who-bee-la-see-**ON**

English	Español	Guide
Severance pay	Indemnización por despedida	in-dem-knee-za-see-**ON** pour days-pay-**DEE**-dah
Sick leave	Días pagados por enfermedad	**DEE**-ahs pah-**GA**-dos pour in-fer-me-**DAD**
Social security	Seguro social	say-**GOO**-row so-see-**AL**
Taxes	Impuestos	em-poo-**ACE**-toes
Tax deductions	Deducciones de impuestos	day-dook-see-**ON**-aces day em-poo-**ACE**-toes
Unemployment Insurance	Seguro de desempleo	say-**GOO**-row day dase-em-**PLAY**-oh
Worker's Compensation	Compensación de obrero	com-pen-za-see-**ON** day o-**BRAY**-row

Para Practicar

You are going through your school's benefit package with Señora Arózqueta. Circle the word in each list that you will want to mention.

1. Madre   Beneficios   Niño

2. Seguro   Estar   Visitar

3. Tía   Ir   Jubilación

4. Necesitar   Paga   Ser

5. Padre   Mirar   Impuestos

6. Seguro social   Observar   Algebra

7. Biblioteca   Vacaciones pagadas   Habla

Answer Key: 1. Beneficios 2. Seguro 3. Jubilación 4. Paga 5. Impuestos 6. Seguro social 7. Vacaciones pagadas

On the Teléfono

Talking on the telephone with Spanish-speaking parents is one of the most challenging skills to develop. There's no body language or facial expressions to help you. The best way to start this process is to stay as organized as possible. Think carefully about the kind of calls you make to your English speaking customers. What are the phrases you say most often? What are the typical responses you hear from parents? These are the kinds of phrases you should learn first. Remember it better to use some of the phrases from page eleven to help you if you get in a jam. There's nothing wrong with saying, *"Repeta, por favor. Habla más despacio."* Make a script to help you get started with telephone skills. This will help you build your confidence.

English	Español	Guide
800 number	Número de ochocientos	**NEW**-may-row day **OH**-cho-see-**N**-toes
Answering machine	Contestador telefónico	con-tes-**TA**-door tay-lay-**FOE**-knee-co
Area code	Código de área	**CO**-d-go day **AH**-ray-ah
Cellular phone	Teléfono celular El cel	tay-lay-**FOE**-no say-**YOU**-lar el cell
Conference call	Llamada de conferencia	ya-**MA**-da de con-fer-**WRENN**-see-ah
Extension	Extensión	x-ten-see-**ON**
Fax	Facsímil	fax-**SEE**-meal
Headset	Auriculares con micrófono	ow-ree-coo-**LAR**-ace con me-**CROW**-foe-no
Switchboard	Conmutador	con-moo-ta-**DOOR**
Telephone number	Número de teléfono	**NEW**-may-row day tay-**LAY**-foe-no
Two-way radio	Radioteléfono portátil	ra-d-oh-tay-**LAY**-foe-no pour-**TA**-teel

More Phrases for the Teléfono

English	Español	Guide
Ask for this number.	Pida este número.	p-da **ES**-tay **NEW**-may-row
Collect call	Llamada a cobro revertido	ya-**MA**-da ah **CO**-bro ray-ver-**T**-doe
Could you call later?	¿Puede llamar más tarde?	poo-**A**-day ya-**MAR** mas **TAR**-day
Dial this number.	Marque este número.	**MAR**-que **ES**-tay **NEW**-may-row
Hang up the telephone.	Cuelgue el teléfono.	coo-**L**-gay el tay-**LAY**-foe-no
He/She isn't here.	No está aquí.	no es-**TA** ah-**KEY**
He/she will call back later.	Llamará más tarde.	ya-**MAR**-rah **MAS** tar-**DAY**
Hold a moment,	Espere un momento, por favor.	es-**PEAR**-ray oon mo-**MEN**-toe pour fa-**VOR**
I have the wrong number.	Tengo el número equivocado.	**TANG**-go el **NEW**-may-row a-key-vo-**CA**-doe
I'd like to leave a message.	Me gustaría dejar un mensaje.	may goo-star-**REE**-ah day-**HAR** oon men-**SA**-je
I'll transfer you to ____	Le voy a transferir a ____	lay voy a trans-fair-**REAR** ah
I'm calling about____.	Estoy llamando acerca de ____.	es-**TOY** ya-**MAHN**-doe ah-**SER**-ca day
Is this the correct number?	¿Es el número correcto?	es el **NEW**-may-row co-**WRECK**-toe
It's very important.	Es muy importante.	es mooy m-pour-**TAHN**-tay
Local call	Llamada local	ya-**MA**-da low-**CAL**
Long distance	Larga distancia	**LAR**-ga dees-**TAN**-see-ah
May I speak to _____?	¿Puedo hablar con ____?	poo-**A**-doe ah-**BLAR** con ____

English	Español	Guide
Press this number.	Oprima este número.	oh-**PRE**-ma **ES**-tay **NEW**-may-row
Repeat that please.	Repítelo, por favor	ray-**P**-tay-low pour fa-**VOR**
The connection is bad.	La conexión está mala.	la co-nex-see-**ON** es-**TA** **MA**-la
The line is busy.	La línea está ocupada.	la **LEE**-nay-ah es-**TA** oh-coo-**PA**-da
The number is disconnected.	El número está desconectada.	el **NEW**-may-row es-**TA** des-co-neck-**TA**-da
There is a phone call for	Hay una llamada para ____.	eye **OO**-na ya-**MA**-da **PA**-ra ____.
Wait for the tone.	Espere por el tono.	es-**PEAR**-ray pour el **TOE**-no
Would you like to leave a message?	¿Le gustaría dejar un mensaje?	lay goo-star-**REE**-ah day-**HAR** oon men-**SA**-he
You have the wrong number.	Tiene el número equivocado.	t-**N**-a l **NEW**-may-row a-key-vo-**CA**-doe
Your name, please	Su nombre, por favor	sue **NOM**-brey pour fa-**VOR**
Your number, please	Su número, por favor	sue **NEW**-may-row pour fa-**VOR**

Para Practicar

Elena Casador's mother calls the school to leave a message for her teacher Ms Cobb. Tell her the following.

1. I'm Mrs. Alran the receptionist. _____

2. Your name, please _____

3. I speak a little Spanish. _____

4. What is your telephone number? _____

5. The line is busy. _____

6. Would you like to leave a message? _____

_____

Instructions - Instrucciones

Here are some common instructions for the workplace. Whether you are behind the counter, speaking with school employees or parents, these phrases will help you communicate in a variety of situations. Don't forget to add *gracias* or *por favor* at the beginning or at the end of the phrase.

English	Español	Guide
Come here.	Venga aquí.	**VEN**-ga ah-**KEY**.
Let's go.	Vámonos.	**VA**-mo-nos
Go with him.	Vaya con él.	**VA**-ya con **L**
Wait	Espere.	ace-**PEAR**-ray
Stop.	Pare.	**PAR**-ray
Help me.	Ayúdeme.	ay-**U**-day-may
Help him.	Ayúdelo.	ay-**U**-day-low
Like this.	Así.	ah-**SEE**
Not like this.	Así no.	ah-**SEE** no
Show me.	Muéstreme.	moo-**ACE**-tray-may
Good.	Bien.	b**N**
Point to it.	Indíquelo.	n-**DEE**-kay-low
Move that here.	Mueve eso aquí.	moo-wavy **ACE**-so ah-**KEY**
Bring me that.	Tráigame eso.	try-**GA**-may **ACE**-toe
Give it to me.	Démelo.	**DAY**-may-low
To the right	A la derecha.	a la day-**RAY**-cha
To the left.	A la izquierda.	a la ees-kay-**AIR**-da
Remove these.	Quite estos.	**KEY**-tay **ACE**-toes
Pick up all these.	Recoja todo estos.	ray-**CO**-ha **TOE**-dos **ES**-toes
Put it there.	Póngalo allí.	**PON**-ga-low ah-**YE**
Around	Alrededor	al-ray-day-**DOOR**
Inside	Dentro	**DEN**-tro
Under	Debajo	day-**BA**-ho
Carry this.	Lleve esto.	**YEA**-vay **ACE**-toe

English	Español	Guide
Open/close	Abra, cierre	**AH**-bra. **SER**-ray
Do it now.	Hágalo ahora.	**AH**-ga-low ah-**ORA**
Do it later.	Hágalo más tarde.	**AH**-ga-low mas **TAR**-day
Here, there	Aquí, allí	ah-**KEY**, ah-**YE**
A little, a lot	Un poco, mucho	un **PO**-ko, **MOO**-cho

Para Practicar

Use the phrases above in combination with the appliances and rooms of the house to say the following:

1. Go with Pablo and help him. _____

2. I need the book (el libro) on the right. _____

3. Move the desk (el escritorio) there. _____

4. Please do it now. _____

5. Help me. ._____

6. Close the door (la puerta). _____

7. Turn off the radio (la radio). _____

8. Go to the front. ._____

9. Work with Esteban._____

Tips & Tidbits

In English it's common to say, "Do you understand my directions? In Spanish, remember to always use the word **instructions** instead of **directions.** This could be confusing to some Latinos because the word *dirección* in español can mean *address!* It's a good idea to ask this simple question: *¿Comprende mis instrucciones?* Also, don't forget to add *por favor* or please to your *instrucciones!*

In the Classroom - En la Sala de Clase

Educational opportunities vary from country to country in Latin America. In many rural areas kindergartens are not available or assessable to each child. The educational experience you provide could very well be their first one. So, it's important for you to get them started out on the right foot.

Remember that even if the child has attended primary school before, the equipment and technology options found there are usually limited. Here's a tip to help you get started. Label the most common items in your classroom in both *inglés* and *español*. It can be a great learning activity for everyone. This will be a big help to your new students, because it will make them feel welcome and accepted. It also sends a positive signal to everyone else in your class that it's fun to learn words in another language.

English	Español	Guide
Aisle	Pasillo	pa-**SEE**-yo
Bell	Campana	cam-**PAN**-na
Book	Libro	**LEE**-bro
Box	Caja	**CA**-ha
Brush	Brocha	**BRO**-cha
Bulletin board	Tablero de anuncios	tab-**LAY**-row day ah-**NUN**-see-ohs
Calculator	Calculadora	cal-coo-la-**DOOR**-rah
Calendar	Calendario	ca-len-**DAR**-ree-oh
Card	Tarjeta	tar-**HEY**-ta
Cassette player	Tocador de casetes	toe-ca-**DOOR** day ca-**SAY**-tays
Chair	Silla	**SEE**-ya
Chalk	Tiza	**TEE**-sa
Chalkboard	Pizarrón	p-sa-**RON**
Chart	Diagrama	d-ah-**GRAM**-ma
Clock	Reloj	**RAY**-low
Closet	Gabinete	ga-bee-**NAY**-tay

English	Español	Guide
Computer	Computadora	com-poo-ta-**DOOR**-rah
Desk	Escritorio	es-cre-**TOE**-ree-oh
Dictionary	Diccionario	dixie-oh-**NAR**-ree-oh
Drawer	Cajón	ca-**HONE**
Electrical outlet	Enchufe	n-**CHEW**-fay
Encyclopedia	Enciclopedia	n-see-clo-**PAY**-dee-an
Eraser	Borrador	bore-ra-**DOOR**
Film	Película	pay-**LEE**-coo-la
Flag	Bandera	ban-**DAY**-rah
Folder	Libreta	lee-**BRAY**-ta
Globe	Mundo	**MOON**-doe
Glue	Pegamento	pay-ga-**MEN**-toe
Group	Grupo	**GREW**-po
Headphones	Audífonos	ow-**DEE**-foe-nos
Intercom	Interfono	n-ter-**FOE**-no
Loudspeaker	Altoparlante	**AL**-toe-par-**LAN**-tay
Map	Mapa	**MA**-pa
Marker	Marcador	mark-ah-**DOOR**
Notebook	Cuaderno	coo-ah-**DARE**-no
Page	Página	**PA**-he-na
Paint	Pintura	peen-**TOO**-rah
Paper	Papel	pa-**PELL**
Pen	Lapicero	la-pee-**SAY**-row
Pencil	Lápiz	**LA**-pees
Pencil sharpener	Sacapuntas	sa-ca-**POON**-tas
Projector	Proyector	pro-yec-**TOR**
Row	Fila	**FEE**-la
Ruler	Regla	**RAY**-gla
Sheet of paper	Hoja de papel	**OH**-ha day pa-**PELL**
Stapler	Engrapadora	n-gra-pa-**DOOR**-rah
String	Hilo	**EE**-low
Teacher	Maestro (m) / maestra (f)	my-**A**-stro my-**A**-stra
Teacher's desk	Escritorio del maestro	es-cree-**TOR**-ree-oh del my-**A**-stro

English	Español	Guide
Television	Televisor	tay-lay-**VEE**-soar
Thumbtack	Tachuela	ta-chew-**A**-la
Trash can	Cesto de basura	**SAY**-sto day ba-**SUE**-rah
VCR	Vídeo casetera	**VEE**-day-oh ca-say-**TER**-rah
Video	Vídeo	**VEE**-day-oh

Giving Directions: In Spanish the word dirección means address, so using it when you are giving instructions can be confusing to children. Try to use the word instruction instead. It's almost the same between our two languages. In English say instruction, and in Spanish the word is instrucción. Can you see that they are similar?

Another Tip: Some items in the classroom don't translate well into Spanish. For items like "el Post-it® Note," "el Whiteout®," or "el Kleenex" it's perfectly OK to use "Spanglish." These items enjoy strong name brand recognition throughout the world.

Para Practicar

Using phrases from the chapter on "instructions," the números, and the "sweet 16 verbs" write the following phrases in Spanish.

1. Come to the board. _____

2. You need your book. _____

3. You need a brush. _____

4. Go to the pencil sharpener. _____

5. Where is your group? _____

6. Page 25 _____

7. Where is your pencil? _____

8. You need your paper. _____

9. Use the paint. _____

10. Prepare your folder. _____

Tips and Tidbits

As an educator, it's important for you to realize that many of your students may be hearing and speaking only Spanish at home. Even though many Latinos are bilingual, Spanish is the primary language used at home. It's always more comfortable to speak one's native language in that setting. Learning two languages in childhood is a natural process. Early in the year your Hispanic student could fall behind while he or she is improving in English. Give them all the help and support you can. By the end of the year you will be amazed at their progress!

Classroom Instructions
Instrucciones en la sala de clase

Giving instructions in the classroom is always a necessary and important part of teaching; however, there are some cultural differences that you should be aware of when you are working with Spanish speaking students. Courtesy is an important part of the Spanish language and its culture. Two of the most important words in Spanish are thank you and please. To earn the respect of your students, use gracias and por favor often, and don't forget to add a big smile!

English	Español	Guide
Sit down *(pl)*	¡Siéntense!	see-**N**-tay-say
Stand up	¡Levántese!	lay-**VAN**-tay-say
Behave	¡Pórtate bien!	**POUR**-ta-tay bn
Pay attention	¡Presta atención!	**PRAY**-stay ah-ten-see-**ON**
Line up *(pl)*	¡Pónganse en fila!	**PON**-gan-say n **FEE**-la
Turn around	¡Date vuelta!	**DA**-tay voo-**EL**-ta
Be quiet	¡Silencio!	see-**LEN**-see-oh
Ask permission *(pl)*	¡Pidan permiso!	**PEE**-dahn pear-**ME**-so
Only one person at a time speaks.	Solo una persona hable a la vez.	**SO**-low **OO**-na pear-**SO**-na **AH**-blay ah la vase
Please raise your hand.	Levanta la mano, por favor.	lay-**VAN**-ta la **MA**-no Pour fa-**VOR**
Please wait your turn.	Tienes que esperar tu turno, por favor.	t-**N**-ace ka es-pear-**RAR** to **TOUR**-no pour fa-**VOR**
Don't push.	¡No empuje!	No m-**POO**-hey
Come here	Venga aquí.	**VEIN**-gah ah-**KEY**
Wait	Espere	es-**PEAR** ray
Watch	Mire	**MIR**-ray

English	Español	Guide
Stop!	¡Párese!	**PA**-ray-say
Hurry up!	¡Apúrate!	ah-**POO**-rah-tay
Where are you going?	¿Adónde va?	ah-**DON**-day vah
What do you need?	¿Qué necesita?	kay nay-say-**SEE**-ta
What's the problem?	¿Cuál es el problema?	coo-**AL** es 1 pro-**BLAY**-ma
I'm going to call your parents.	Voy a telefonear a sus padres.	voy ah tay-lay-phone-a-**ARE** ah seus **PA**-drays

Remember that the word "no" in English is the same thing in Spanish. You can start several of your instructions with it. Add "por favor" at the end, to give what you say a more courteous tone. In many of these phrases it's fine to use the verb infinitive. That makes this type of command "muy fácil."

English	Español	Guide
No…	No...	No
Bothering others	Molestar a los demás	mo-lace-**TAR** ah los day-**MAS**
Fighting	Pelear	pay-lay-**ARE**
Gum chewing	Masticar chicle	mas-tee-**CAR** **CHEEK**-lay
Hitting	Pegar	pay-**GAR**
Kicking	Patear	pa-tay-**ARE**
Littering	Tirar basura	tee-**RAR** ba-**SUE**-rah
Pushing	Empujar	m-poo-**HAR**
Run	Correr	**CORE**-rah
Skipping class	Faltar a la clase	fal-**TAR** ah la **CLA**-say
Smoking	Fumar	foo-**MAR**
Spitting	Escupir	es-coo-**PIER**
Throwing things	Tirar cosas	tee-**RAR** **CO**-sas
Tripping	Tropezar	tro-pay-**SAR**
Yelling	Gritar	gree-**TAR**

Cultural Information - Información Cultural

Male and female roles are often clearly defined and much more traditional in Latin America than they are in the United States. Women often stay at home, taking care of the residence and the children. Men work outside the home and take care of much of the financial responsibilities for the family. So, from an early age, children are taught to perform specific tasks, while other tasks are left for those of the opposite sex. This is particularly true with household chores. Cleaning up and cooking are chores that are still done primarily by women. Things that are expected of young men are quite different from what is expected of young ladies. It's important to be aware of these cultural differences. Try to be patient, especially if one of your students refuses to perform a certain task. Give them some time; soon they will learn to make their own decisions.

Para Practicar
Your class is going to a play in the school theater. Give these instructions:

Line up. _____

Be quiet. _____

Don't bother others. _____

Carlos is causing problems in class. Remind him of the following school rules.

No fighting. _____

No kicking. _____

No spitting. _____

I'm going to call your parents. _____

Around the School — Alrededor la Escuea

Schools in America offer so much diversity in both courses and activities. Unless your Spanish-speaking student has been able to go to a modern, urban school, many of the areas on your campus will be different to them. Use these words to take them on a complete tour of your campus or *el campo*.

English	Español	Guide
Administration	Administración	ad-men-knee-stra-see-**ON**
Auditorium	Auditorio	ow-dee-**TOR**-ree-oh
Cafeteria	Cafetería	ca-fay-ter-**REE**-ah
Classroom	Sala de clase	sal-la day **CLA**-day
Counselor's Office	Oficina de la consejera	oh-fee-**SEE**-na day con-say-**HEY**-rah
Courtyard	Plaza	**PLA**-sa
Entrance	Entrada	n-**TRA**-da
Gym	Gimnasio	him-**NA**-see-oh
Hall	Corredor	core-ray-**DOOR**
Laboratory	Laboratorio	la-bore-ra-**TOR**-ree-oh
Library	Biblioteca	b-blee-oh-**TEK**-ah
Lobby	Vestíbulo	vest-**T**-boo-low
Locker	Armario	are-**MAR**-ree-oh
Office	Oficina	of-fee-**SEEN**-ah
Parking lot	Estacionamiento	es-ta-see-on-na-me-**N**-toe
Playground	Campo de recreo	**CAM**-po day ray-**CRAY**-oh
Restroom	Baño *or* Servicio	**BA**-nyo ser-**V**-see-oh
Theatre	Teatro	tay-**AH**-tro
Workshop	Taller	ta-**YER**
First floor	Primer piso	pre-**MARE P**-so
Second floor	Segundo piso	say-**GOON**-doe **P**-so

English	Español	Guide
Third floor	Tercero piso	ter-**SAY**-row P-so
Exit	Salida	sa-**LEE**-da
Stairs	Escaleras	es-ca-**LAIR**-rah
Left	Izquierda	es-key-**AIR**-duh
Right	Derecha	day-**RAY**-cha
Up	Arriba	ah-**REE**-ba
Down	Abajo	ah-**BA**-ho
Far	Lejos	**LAY**-hos
Near	Cerca	**SER**-ka
Beside	Al lado	al **LA**-doe
Outside	Afuera	ah-foo-**AIR**-rah
Department	Departamento	day-par-ta-**MEN**-toe

Para Practicar

Here is a list of important connecting words. Use them to give the following directions and instructions:

To = A la (f) & Al (m)   From = De la (f) & Del (m)

1. Go to the counselor's office. _____

2. We are going to the auditorium. _____

3. Go to your locker. _____

4. The cafeteria is beside the office. _____

5. Your class is on the second floor. _____

6. The gym is to the right of the theatre. _____

7. The bathroom is beside the stairs. _____

8. Wait in the lobby. _____

9. The exit is to the left. _____

10. The library is on the third floor. _____

The School Staff — Los Empleados de la Escuela

One of the differences between English and Spanish is the practice of dividing nouns into two categories. This is can be a confusing concept for us since words aren't divided into gender categories in English. *Words in Spanish are not divided into categories because of what they mean. They are separated into categories by how they sound.* So, even though a chair or a *silla* is put into the feminine category, you can't give it feminine qualities. Because it's a thing, it can't have any feminine qualities! Most words that end with the letter "a" are put into the feminine category. Of course, there are some exceptions. Languages are very much like the people who use them. We don't always follow the rules! With people and their professions this becomes an easy difference to learn. It's also very practical. For some of the jobs around the school listed below, you will see two choices. The second word that ends with an "a" is for a lady who performs that job. When you introduce her, put "*la*" in front of what she does. When you are introducing a man, "*el*" goes in front of his profession. If there is only one listing, that word can be used for either a man or a woman.

English	Español	Guide
Bus driver	Chofer del autobús	cho-**FAIR** del ow-toe-**BOOS**
Cashier	Cajero / cajera	ca-**HAIR**-row
Counselor	Consejero / consejera	con-say-**HEY**-row
Crossing guard	Guardia del tráfico	goo-**ARE**-dee-ah del **TRAH**-fee-co
Employees	Empleados	m-play-**AH**-does
Interpreter	Intérprete	n-**TER**-pray-tay
Janitor	Bedel	bay-**DELL**
Librarian	Bibliotecario Bibliotecaria	b-blee-oh-tek-**ARE**-ree-oh b-blee-oh-tek-**ARE**-ree-ah

English	Español	Guide
Nurse	Enfermero	n-fer-**MAY**-row
	Enfermera	n-fer-**MAY**-rah
Personnel	Personal	pear-so-**NAL**
Police	Policía	po-lee-**SEE**-ah
Principal	Director	dee-wreck-**TOR**
	Directora	dee-wreck-**TOR**-rah
Psychologist	Psicólogo	see-**CO**-low-go
	Psicóloga	see-**CO**-low-ga
Receptionist	Recepcionista	ray-cep-see-on-**KNEE**-sta
Secretary	Secretario	sec-ray-**TAR**-ree-oh
	Secretaria	sec-ray-**TAR**-ree-ah
Security guard	Guardia de seguridad	goo-**ARE**-dee-ah day Say-goo-ree-**DAD**
Specialist	Especialista	es-pay-see-al-**EAST**-ta
Staff	Funcionarios	foon-see-oh-**NAR**-ree-ohs
Superintendent	Superintendente	soup-pear-n-ten-**DEN**-tay
Teacher	Maestro	may-**A**-stro
	Maestra	may-**A**-stra
Teacher's aide	Ayudante	eye-oo-**DAN**-tay
	Ayudanta de maestro	eye-oo-**DAN**-tay day may-**A**-stro
Translator	Traductor	trah-duke-**TOR**
	Traductora	trah-duke-**TOR**-rah
Vice-principal	Subdirector	soob-dee-wreck-**TOR**
	Subdirectora	soob-dee-wreck-**TOR**-rah
Volunteer	Voluntario	vol-oon-**TAR**-ree-oh
	Voluntaria	vol-oon-**TAR**-ree-ah

Para Practicar

You are taking Fernando, new student from El Salvador, on a tour of your school. Building relationships is an important part of Latin American culture, so it's important to introduce everyone you meet around the campus. To practice this skill, say what people do in Spanish to yourself as you meet them during the day! This is a great way to incorporate practice into your day!

Use the following as an example. Mrs. Roberts is the receptionist. Señora Roberts es la receptionista.

**Pronounce your colleague's name as you normally do, but do add Spanish courtesy titles.

1. Mr. Farmer is the principal.

   _____.

2. Miss Braxton is the vice-principal.

   _____.

3. Mrs. Pearson is the crossing guard.

   _____.

4. Mr. Gonzáles is the interpreter.

   _____.

5. Mrs. Fong is the bus driver.

   _____.

6. Miss Sigmon is the teacher's aid.

   _____.

7. Mr. Patterson is the counselor.

   _____.

8. Mrs. Causby is the teacher.

   _____.

Subjects - Sujetos

Schools around the world teach the basics of reading, writing, and arithmetic. So some of the subjects you offer at your *escuela* will be the same ones that are offered in other countries. Your Hispanic students will be familiar with those basics. However, most US schools offer a variety of elective subjects that aren't found in Latin American schools. This list should be easy to learn because there are lots of *cognates*. These are words that are almost identical in both languages. What *sujetos* do you **enseña**?

English	Español	Guide
Achievement test	Prueba de rendimiento	pru-**A**-ba day ren-d-mee-**N**-toe
Algebra	Álgebra	**AL**-hey-bra
Art	Arte	**ARE**-tay
Assignment	Trabajo	tra-**BAH**-ho
Biology	Biología	b-oh-low-**HE**-ha
Calculus	Cálculo	**CAL**-coo-low
Chemistry	Química	**KEY**-me-ca
Chorus	Coro	**CORE**-oh
Civics	Civismo	c-**VEES**-mo
Computers	Computadoras	com-poo-ta-**DOOR**-ahs
Drama	Drama	**DRA**-ma
Driver's education	Enseñanza de conducir	n-sen-**YAN**-sa day con-doo-**SEER**
Earth science	Ciencia de la tierra	c-**N**-see-ah day la t-**AIR**-ah
End of grade	Final de grado	fee-**NAL** day **GRAH**-do
End of semester	Final de semestre	fee-**NAL** day say-**MAY**-stra
English as a second language	Ingles cómo segundo idioma	eng-**LACE CO**-mo say-**GOON**-doe e-dee-**OH**-ma

English	Español	Guide
Failed	Retenido	ray-tay-**NEE**-do
Foreign language	Idiomas extranjeros	e-dee-**OH**-mas x-tran-**HAIR**-ros
French	Francés	fran-**SAYS**
Geography	Geografía	hey-oh-gra-**FEE**-ah
Geometry	Geometría	hey-oh-may-**TREE**-ah
Grade level	Nivel de grado	knee-**VEL** day **GRAH**-do
Health	Salud	sa-**LEWD**
History	Historia	ees-**TOR**-ree-ah
Homework	Tarea	tar-**RAY**-ah
I.E.P.	Plan educativo individual	plahn ed-u-ca-**TEE**-vo in-dee-vid-u-**AL**
Industrial arts	Artes industriales	**ARE**-tays n-do-stree-**AL**-ace
Keyboarding	Escritura a máquina	es-scree-**TO**-rah ah **MA**-key-na
Language arts	Lenguaje	len-goo-**AH**-hey
Latin	Latín	la-**TEEN**
Literature	Literatura	lee-ter-rah-**TO**-rah
Mathematics	Matemáticas	ma-tay-**MA**-tee-cas
Music	Música	**MOO**-see-ca
Physical education	Educación física	a-do-ca-see-**ON** **FEE**-see-ca
Physics	Física	**FEE**-see-ca
Placement test	Examen de nivel	x-**AH**-men day knee-**VEL**
Promoted	Promovido	pro-mo-**VEE**-do
Reading	Lectura	lec-**TOO**-rah
Social studies	Estudios sociales	es-**TO**-dee-ohs so-see-**AL**-ace
Special education	Educación especial	a-do-ca-see-**ON** es-pay-see-**AL**
Speech	Discurso	dees-**COOR**-so
Subject	Sujeto	sue-**HEY**-to
Test	Examen	x-**AH**-men

English	Español	Guide
US History	Historia de los Estados Unidos	Ees-**TOR**-ree-ah de los Ace-**TA**-dos oo-**KNEE**-dos
World History	Historia mundial	ees-**TOR**-ree-ah moon-dee-**AL**
Writing	Escritura	es-scree-**TO**-rah

Para Practicar

In the last chapter we discussed the school staff. Think about the instructors on your staff and introduce them to Elena, a student from Honduras. When you introduce your colleagues, start with the word for teacher, maestro or maestra. Next add the word "de" and follow it by the subject they instruct. Use the following as a guide:

Mrs. Stewart is the physical education teacher.
Señora Stewart es la maestra de educación física.

Mrs. Young is the reading teacher.

_____.

Miss Rocket is the algebra teacher.

_____.

Mrs. Kidd is the English teacher.

_____.

Mr. McIntosh is the geometry teacher.

_____.

Mr. Taylor is the biology teacher.

_____.

Mr. Epeley is the French teacher.

_____.

Mrs. Frick is the Latin teacher.

_____.

Mr. Alonso is the music teacher.

_____.

Now that you have introduced Elena to some of the instructors at your school, she needs to know what courses to take. Plan her course of study. She's in the 9th grade.

Elena, you need to take an algebra class.
Elena, necesita inscribirse en una clase de algebra.

You need to take a history class.

_____.

You need to take English as a Second Language.

_____.

You need to take a physical education class.

_____.

You need to take a civics class.

_____.

You need to take a math class.

_____.

You need to take a music class.

_____.

You need to take writing.

_____.

You need to take US History.

_____.

You need to take algebra.

_____.

You need to take speech.

_____.

You need to take a placement test.

_____.

You need to take literature.

_____.

The Counselor
El Consejero or La Consejera

Teachers, administrators, and counselors often have to discuss very sensitive subjects with their students. Sometimes students with personal problems or "problemas personales," are more comfortable discussing issues with you rather than their parents. This is such an important role and because of the challenges presented by language, it can be difficult! Before you see your students, look up important words that will help you get started. Try to anticipate what you will need to say and have those phrases handy. Get started by learning the topics listed below, but to discuss these issues in detail, you will probably need the help of a translator.

English	Español	Guide
Absences	Ausencias	ow-**SEN**-see-ahs
Abuse	Abuso	ah-**BOO**-so
Accident	Accidente	ax-see-**DENT**-tay
Alcohol	Alcohol	al-co-**OL**
Argument	Discusión	dees-coo-see-**ON**
Cigarettes	Cigarrillos	see-gar-**REE**-yos
Confrontation	Confrontación	con-fron-ta-see-**ON**
Drugs	Drogas	**DRO**-gas
Fight	Pelea	pay-**LAY**-ah
Harassment	Acosamiento	ah-co-sa-me-**N**-toe
Illness	Enfermedad	n-fer-may-**DAD**
Injury	Herida	air-**REE**-da
Personal hygiene	Higiene personal	e-he-**N**-ay pear-so-**NAL**
Pregnancy	Embarazo	m-bar-**AH**-so
Tardiness	Tardanzas	tar-**DAN**-sas
Threat	Amenaza	ah-men-**NA**-sa

Para Practicar
Tell Margarita that you need to discuss the following issues. For the word your use "tu" for the singular and "tus" for the plural.

I need to discuss_____.   Necesito discutir _____.

Your absences _____

Your alcohol _____

Your fight _____

Your cigarettes _____

Your threat _____

Your illness _____

Your argument _____

Your drugs _____

Your problem _____

Your tardiness _____

64

Feelings - Sentimientos

Discussing how a student feels is a very important part of counseling. Even though kids often wear their feelings on their faces, it can be difficult to get them to open up—especially if there is a language barrier. Here is a list of common emotions that will help you begin a dialogue. Don't forget to change the last letter from an "o" to an "a" when you are talking with girls. Your Hispanic student could be very shy when you begin. Be patient, go slowly and build the rapport you need.

English	Español	Guide
Afraid	Asustado	ah-seus-**TA**-doe
Angry	Enojado	ay-no-**HA**-doe
Bored	Aburrido	ah-boo-**REE**-doe
Confused	Confundido	con-foon-**DEE**-doe
Depressed	Deprimido	day-pre-**ME**-doe
Discontent	Descontento	des-con **TENT**-oh
Distracted	Distraído	dees-tra-**EE**-doe
Embarrassed	Turbado	tour-**BA**-doe
Frustrated	Frustrado	froo-**STRA**-doe
Furious	Furioso	fur-ree-**OH**-so
Guilty	Culpable	cool-**PA**-blay
Happy	Feliz	fay-**LEASE**
Hated	Odiado	oh-dee-**AH**-doe
Impatient	Impaciente	m-pa-see-**N**-tay
Inferior	Inferior	een-fair-ree-**OR**
Nervous	Nervioso	ner-vee-**OH**-so
Restless	Inquieto	een-key-**A**-toe
Sad	Triste	**TREE**-stay
Sick	Enfermo	n-**FAIR**-mo
Tense	Tenso	**TEN**-so
Trapped	Atrapado	ah-tra-**PA**-doe
Uncomfortable	Incómodo	een-**CO**-mo-doe
Worried	Preocupado	pray-oh-coo-**PA**-doe

Para Practicar
Jorge has come to your office to discuss a problem with his grades. Ask about his feelings.

Are you _____?   *¿Estás _____?*

1. Frustrated _____

2. Worried _____.

3. Bored _____.

4. Depressed _____.

5. Nervous _____.

6. Sad   _____.

7. Uncomfortable _____

8. Impatient _____.

9. Tense _____.

10..Confused _____.

11.Restless _____.

12.Tense _____.

13.Distracted _____.

14.Sick _____

15.Afraid _____

The Advice - El Consejo

Even though you might need an interpreter to help you get to the bottom of some problems, you could very well be on the front line. By using your Spanish as much as possible, you will put both students and their parents at ease. Just try your best! Here are some phrases that will help you grab hold of the situation.

Start each of these phrases with *"favor de"* to mean please. That phrase can always be followed by a verb infinitive. That makes these phrases easy to use.

English	Español	Guide
Breathe deeply	Respirar profundamente	ray-spear-**RAR** pro-foon-da-**MEN**-tay
Call your doctor	Llamar a tu doctor	ya-**MAR** ah too doc-**TOR**
Calm down	Calmarse	cal-**MAR**-say
Change your schedule	Cambiar tu horario	cam-bee-**ARE** too or-**RARE**-ree-oh
Come back later	Regresar más tarde	ray-grey-**SAR** mas **TAR**-day
Go to class	Ir a tu clase	ear ah too **CLAH**-say
Lower your voice	Bajar la voz	baa-**HAR** la vos
Pay attention	Prestar atención	pray-**STAR** ah-ten-see-**ON**
Sleep more	Dormir más	door-**MIR** mas
Stay away from them	Apartarte de ellos	ah-**PAR**-ta-tay day **A**-yos
Take your medicine	Tomar tu medicina	to-**MAR** too may-dee-**SEEN**-ah
Tell your family	Decirle a tu familia	day-**SEAR**-lay ah too fa-**ME**-lee-ah
Visit a specialist	Visitar un especialista	v-see-**TAR** oon es-pay-see-al-**EES**-ta

English	Español	Guide
Please don't	Favor de no	fa-**VOR** day no
Argue	Discutir	dees-coo-**TEAR**
Bother	Molestar	mo-lace-**TAR**
Curse	Usar profanidad	oo-**SAR** pro-fan-knee-**DAD**
Joke	Bromear	bro-may-**ARE**
Lie	Mentir	men-**TIER**
Tease	Burlarte	boor-**LAR**-tay

Important Questions - Preguntas Importantes

Listening is a very important part of both counseling and teaching. Asking the right questions can be just as important. Remember to keep your questions brief and to the point. Go back to the phrases on page twelve if you don't understand what's being said to you. Here's a short list to help you get started.

English	Español	Guide
Are you OK?	¿Estás bien?	es-**TAS** b-n
Are you sick?	¿Estás enfermo? ¿Estás enferma?	es -**TAS** n-**FER**-mo es -**TAS** n-**FER**-ma
What is the problem?	¿Cuál es el problema?	coo-**AL** es l pro-**BLAY**-ma
Do you need help?	¿Necesitas ayuda?	nay-say-**SEE**-tas eye-**YOU**-da
Do you need to speak with me?	¿Necesitas hablarme?	nay-say-**SEE**-tas ah-**BLAR**-may
What happened?	¿Qué pasó?	kay pa-**SO**
Do you have information?	¿Tienes información?	t-N-ace n-for-ma-see-**ON**
When did the problem start?	¿Cuándo empezó el problema?	coo-**AN**-doe m-pay-**SO** L pro-**BLAY**-ma
Did you argue?	¿Discutiste?	dees-coo-**TEES**-tay
Did you refuse?	¿Te negaste?	tay nay-**GAS**-tay
Did you disobey?	¿Desobedeciste?	des-oh-bay-d-**CEASE**-tay

English	Español	Guide
Did you steal?	¿Robaste?	ro-BAAS-tay
Did you lie?	¿Mentiste?	men-TEASE-tay
I need to call your parents.	Necesito llamar a tus padres.	nay-say-SEE-toe ya-MAR Ah tus PA-drays
What is your telephone number?	¿Cuál es tu número de teléfono?	coo-AL es sue NEW-may-row day tay-LAY-fo-no

Para Practicar
What would you say in the following situations? List at least 3 phrases.

1. Rafael was in a fight. _____

_____

2. Celia is sick. _____

_____

3. Juan's grades have dropped. _____

_____

4. Maribel has a problem with one of her teachers. _____

_____

5. Francisco needs help with his math. _____

_____

6. You think that José saw another student steal some lunch money. ___

_____

_____

Motivation — La Motivación

Students appreciate your efforts to encourage and motivate them. This is particularly important for those who have a new language and so many other new things to learn. What a positive aspect of your position within the school! Doesn't it give you a good feeling to be able to encourage and reward good work with positive comments? Let your Hispanic students know how much you appreciate their hard work and determination. A big smile will go a long way when you use these phrases.

English	Español	Guide
It's .....!	¡Es....!	es
Excellent	Excelente	x-see-**LEN**-tay
Fantastic	Fantástico	fan-**TAS**-tee-co
Good	Bueno	boo-**WAY**-no
Incredible	Increíble	n-cray-**E**-blay
Extraordinary	Extraordinario	x-tra-or-dee-**NAR**-ree-oh
Magnificent	Magnífico	mag-**KNEE**-fee-co
What good work!	¡Qué buen trabajo!	kay boo-**WAYNE** tra-**BAA**-ho
Very good!	¡Muy bien!	mooy b-**N**
You're very important!	¡Eres muy importante!	**AIR**-ace mooy m-por-**TAN**-tay
You're very bright!	¡Eres muy brillante!	**AIR**-ace mooy bree-**YAN**-tay
You learn quickly.	Aprendes rápido.	ah-**PREN**-days **RAH**-p-doe
You are smart.	Eres inteligente.	**AIR**-ace n-tell-e-**HEN**-tay
You are responsible.	Eres responsable.	**AIR**-ace ray-spon-**SA**-blay
You are nice.	Eres simpático.	**AIR**-ace seem-**PA**-tee-co
I respect you.	Te respeto.	tay race-**PAY**-toe
You are very valuable.	¡Eres valioso!	**AIR**-ace val-ee-**OH**-so

A Little More— Un Poquíto Más

English	Español	Guide
There is or there are	Hay...	eye
Advancement	Ascenso	ahs-**SEN**-so
Opportunity	Oportunidad	oh-por-too-knee-**DAD**
Great potential	Gran potencial	gran po-ten-see-**AL**
High standards	Normas altas	**NOR**-mas **AL**-tas
Obvious progress	Progreso obvio	Pro-**GRES**-oh ob-**V**-oh
Realistic goals	Metas posibles	**MAY**-tas po-**SEE**-blays
Self-motivation	Motivación personal	Mo-tee-va-see-**ON** Pear-so-**NAL**

Parent Teacher Conferences
La Reunión Entre Los Padres y La Maestra

The family is a very important part of Latin American culture. Families are usually very close and children are considered treasures. The extended family is very important, so when you call for a family conference, you could get several relatives involved. Don't let this make you nervous. Everyone has the child's best interest at heart. It's also important for you to remember that the parents of your Hispanic students could be nervous around you. They might not be comfortable speaking English, just like you aren't comfortable speaking Spanish. Practice what you are going to say before everyone arrives and try to anticipate questions. Don't hesitate to make a "cheat-sheet" with the words and phrases you want 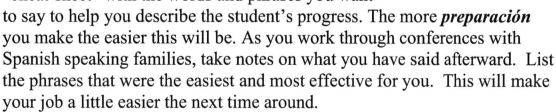 to say to help you describe the student's progress. The more *preparación* you make the easier this will be. As you work through conferences with Spanish speaking families, take notes on what you have said afterward. List the phrases that were the easiest and most effective for you. This will make your job a little easier the next time around.

English	Español	Guide
Please come to the office.	Favor de venir a la oficina.	fa-**VOR** day ven-**EAR** ah la oh-fee-**SEE**-na
I need to talk to you.	Necesito hablar con usted.	nay-say-**SEE**-toe ah-**BLAR** con oo-**STED**
I need to talk about ____.	Necesito hablar de ____.	nay-say-**SEE**-toe ah-**BLAR** day
It's important.	Es importante.	es m-por-**TAN**-tay
It's serious.	Es serio.	es **SAY**-ree-oh
It's urgent.	Es urgente.	es uoor-**HEN**-tay
Please come at (time)	Favor de venir a (time).	fa-**VOR** day ven-**EAR** ah ____

The Positives

Trying to speak Spanish will no doubt you will be a little nervous during your meeting. This is normal. The more practice you have, the less anxiety you will feel. Just prepare in advance and start with the positives!

Give the name of the student and then use "es" or is. If the student you are discussing is a girl, change the ending from "o" to "a." Then, follow up with one of these great adjectives!

English	Español	Guide
Athletic	Atlético	aht-**LAY**-tee-co
Industrious/studious	Aplicado	ah-plea-**CA**-doe
Obedient	Obediente	oh-bay-dee-**N**-tay
Organized	Organizado	or-gan-knee-**SA**-doe
Punctual	Puntual	poon-too-**AL**
Respectful	Respetuoso	ray-**SPEC**-too-oh-so

The Negatives

Try to temper negative statements with positive ones. In Hispanic culture, especially where adults are concerned is in appropriate to give criticism to an individual in a group. That is best done privately. It causes the person to lose face and that's very important. Your constructive criticism could be taken very personally without your even realizing it. Look at the phrases below carefully. In several of them removing the word "no" will really turn things around. Always try to look for strong matches between English and Spanish. This will expand your vocabulary *rápido*.

English	Español	Guide
Cruel	Cruel	crew-**L**
Forgetful	Olvidadizo	ol-vee-da-**DEE**-so
Lazy	Perezoso	pear-ray-**SO**-sew
Rude	Grosero	gro-**SAY**-row
Selfish	Egoísta	a-go-**EES**-ta
Isn't interested	No está interesado	no ace-**TA** n-ter-ray-**SA**-doe
Doesn't study	No estudia	no es-**TOO**-dee-ah
Always arrives late	Siempre llega tarde	see-**M**-pray YEA-ga **TAR**-day
Misses school	Falta a la escuela	**FALL**-ta ah la es-coo-**A**-la
Is failing classes	Está fallando en las clases.	es-**TA** fa-**YAN**-doe n las **CLA**-says

Para Practicar
Write a short script so you could discuss the following topics with parents.

1. Pedro is an excellent student, who is making good progress.

2. Jorge comes to school late and is missing classes.

3. Isabel sets high standards and is self-motivated.

4. Ana is in an accident that is not serious.

5. Pablo is sick and needs a doctor.

6. Juana is failing her classes because she doesn't study.

7. Miguel is organized and has great potential.

8. Call Mr. & Mrs. Hernandez. You need to talk with them about Juan Carlos. You would like them to come to your office at 4:00pm on Tuesday, April 16th. It's not serious. *(Hint: Review the chapters on telling time. Then go to the section on the days of the week and the months of the year.)*

The Exam - El Examen

Testing is important in evaluating a student's progress. Because it is so essential, *la evaluación* can make everyone nervous. At times like these, positive-feedback can go a long way to put everyone at ease and to set a positive atmosphere in the classroom. This is so true in the actual testing phase of the process and discussing *los resultados*. Spanish really shines here. You can say so much using only a short phrase!

English	Español	Guide
Don't be nervous.	No se ponga nervioso.	no say **PON**-ga ner-vee-**OH**-so
It's OK.	Está bien.	es-**TA** bn
Don't worry.	No se preocupe.	no say pray-oh-**COO**-pay
Results	Resultados	ray-sool-**TA**-does
Exam	Examen	x-**AH**-men
Quiz	Concurso	con-**COOR**-so
Test	Prueba	pru-**A**-baa
Instructions	Instrucciones	n-struc-see-**ON**-ace
Scores	Calificaciones	cal-lee-fee-ca-see-**ON**-ace

English	Español	Guide
Report card	Boletín de evaluación	bow-lay-**TEEN** day a-val-oo-ah-see-**ON**
Grades	Notas	**NO**-tas
Points	Puntos	**POON**-toes
Chapters	Capítulos	ca-**P**-too-lows
Units	Unidades	oo-knee-**DAD**-ace
Examples	Ejemplos	ay-**HEMP**-lows
Questions	Preguntas	pray-**GOON**-tas
It's good.	¡Es bueno!	es boo-**WAY**-no
It's high.	¡Es alto!	es **AL**-toe
It's fantastic.	¡Es fantástico!	es fan-**TAS**-t-co
It's excellent.	¡Es excelente!	es x-say-**LENT**-tay
It's better.	Está mejor.	es -**TA** may-**HOR**
It's correct.	Está correcto.	es -**TA** co-**WRECK**-toe
It's average.	Es el promedio.	es l pro-**MAY**-d-oh
It's low.	Es bajo.	es **BAA**-ho
It's unacceptable.	Es inaceptable.	es n-ah-cep **TA**-blay
It's incorrect.	Está incorrecto.	es-**TA** n-co-**WRECK**-toe
It's not good.	No está bueno.	no es -**TA** boo-**WAY**-no
It needs improvement.	Necesita mejorar.	nay-say-**SEE**-ta may-hor-**RAR**
I'm sorry.	Lo siento.	low see-**N**-toe

Para Practicar
What would you say in each of the following situations?

1. You have just finished grading Margarita's test and it's much better than she has ever done before.

2. Roberto has turned in a book report that is promising. You know he can improve.

3. Manuel was late turning in his report. That is unacceptable.

Giving Directions

The ability to give directions in *español* is one of the most practical skills you can have. It adds to your conversational ability and it's a skill you will use over and over again. Slowly, you can start to learn this important vocabulary by knowing simple things, such as the four directions: north, south, east and west. Then, add turns like right and left. Before you know it, you'll be able to give directions to places around town and in your office. This is also easy vocabulary to practice because you can work on it anywhere you go!

English	Español	Guide
Where is it?	¿Dónde está?	**DON**-day ace-**TA**
North	Norte	**NOR**-tay
South	Sur	**SUE**-er
East	Este	**ACE**-tay
West	Oeste	oh-**ACE**-tay
Above	Encima	n-**SEE**-ma
Aisle	Pasillo	pa-**SEE**-yo
Avenue	Avenida	ah-ven-**KNEE**-da
Behind	Detrás	day-**TRAHS**
Down	Abajo	ah-**BAA**-ho
Here	Aquí	ah-**KEY**
In front of	En frente de	n **FREN**-tay day
Inside	Adentro	ah-**DEN**-tro
Near	Cerca	**CER**-ca
Next to	Al lado de	al **LA**-doe day
Outside	Afuera	ah-foo-**AIR**-ah
Over there	Allá	ah-**YA**
Straight ahead	Adelante	ah-day-**LAN**-tay
Street	Calle	ca-**YEA**
There	Allí	ah-**YE**
To the left	A la izquierda	ah la ees-key-**AIR**-dah
Turn	Doble	**DOE**-blay
To the right	A la derecha	ah la day-**RAY**-cha
Up	Arriba	ah-**REE**-ba

Around Town

When Hispanic students enter your school and begin life in a new town, they will want to check out the surrounding area. Knowing vocabulary for places around town will provide you with the kind of terminology that will make you a great *ambassadora*. The next time you go out to run errands around your city or town, check the list below. Where are you going? Make a numbered list of the places you intend to go along with the Spanish words for the directions that will get you there. Now you can practice two important sets of vocabulary at the same time. Also think about grouping this vocabulary into logical sets. Which places involve travel? Which places involve recreation? Which locations do your students ask you about most often? Now, let's get going!

English	Español	Guide
Airport	Aeropuerto	ah-eh-row-poo-**AIR**-toe
Bakery	Panadería	pan-ah-day-**REE**-ah
Bank	Banco	**BAN**-co
Barber shop	Peluquería	pay-loo-kay-**REE**-ah
Beauty salon	Salón de belleza	sa-**LAWN** day bay-**YEA**-sa
Church	Iglesia	e-**GLAY**-see-ah
City hall	Municipio	moon-knee-**SEE**-p-oh
Fire department	Departamento de bomberos	day-par-ta-**MEN**-toe day bom-**BAY**-rows
Florist	Florería	floor-ray-**REE**-ah
Gas station	Gasolinera	gas-so-lee-**NAY**-rah
Grocery store	Grosería	gros-eh-**REE**-ah
Hospital	Hospital	os-p-**TAL**
Hotel	Hotel	oh-**TEL**
Jewelry store	Joyería	hoy-eh-**REE**-ah
Laundromat	Lavandería	la-van-day-**REE**-ah
Library	Biblioteca	b-blee-oh-**TECK**-ah
Market	Mercado	mare-**CA**-doe
Movie theatre	Cine	**SEEN**-nay
Museum	Museo	moo-**SAY**-oh
Park	Parque	**PAR**-kay
Pharmacy	Farmacia	far-**MA**-see-ah

English	Español	Guide
Police station	Estación de policía	es-ta-see-**ON** day po-lee-**SEE**-ah
Post office	Correo	core-**A**-oh
Restaurant	Restaurante	res-tower-**AHN**-tay
School	Escuela	es-coo-**A**-la
Shoe store	Zapatería	sa-pa-tay-**REE**-ah
Store	Tienda	t-**N**-da
Super market	Super Mercado	soo-**PEAR** mare-**CA**-doe
Theatre	Teatro	tay-**AH**-trow
Train station	Estación de tren	es-ta-see-**ON** day tren
Subway	Metro	**MAY**-tro

Para Practicar

Using the list above write down the Spanish names for the places students ask you about frequently.

_____

_____

_____

_____

Tips & Tidbits:

Neither the names of businesses nor the names of streets are translated into Spanish. The proper name of your school should not be translated. In most Latin American cities, numbers and the words street and avenue are commonly used in addresses as they are in most metropolitan areas of the US. It's not uncommon to find 5th Avenue or 52nd Street. But, our neighborhood street, well— that's another story! Street names like Taniger Lane, Red Fox Run, or Wood Stork Cove are impossible to translate from one language to another. You should be aware; however, that sometimes a Spanish-speaking person will give you the number of their street address *en español.* Simple numbers are one of the most important sets of vocabulary you can have!

Para Practicar

Write down the directions to your office from a major landmark in your city. Then write down the directions from the parking lot to your office.

_____

_____

_____

_____

_____

_____

Calming Your Kids

Building good relationships with Latino students and parents makes education an even more worthwhile endeavor. Everyone likes to hear a compliment, especially when it's said from the heart. The path to starting this relationship often begins with a smile and a simple phrase or two. On the following list you will find some great "one-liners" that will help you get started. Practice these often and have fun!
You will get lots of smiles and encouragement from everyone!

English	Español	Guide
Don't worry.	No se preocupe.	no say pray-oh-**COO**-pay
Good luck!	¡Buena suerte!	boo-**WAY**-na **SWEAR**-tay
Take it easy!	¡Cuídese bien!	coo-**E**-day-say b-**N**
Calm down	¡Cálmese!	**CAL**-may-say
How pretty!	¡Qué lindo! (m) ¡Qué linda! (f)	kay **LEAN**-doe kay **LEAN**-da

English	Español	Guide
He's precious! She's precious!	¡Es precioso! ¡Es preciosa!	ace pray-see-**OH**-so ace pray-see-**OH**-sa
What a cute outfit!	¡Qué bonita ropa!	kay bow-**KNEE**-ta **ROW**-pa
What a smile!	¡Qué sonrisa!	kay son-**REE**-sa
It's OK.	Está bien.	ace-**TA** b-N
Have a nice day!	¡Qué le vaya bien! Tenga un buen día.	kay lay **VA**-ya b-N **TEN**-ga oon boo-**WAYNE DEE**-ah
How old is your baby?	¿Cuántos años tiene su bebé?	coo-**AN**-toes **AN**-yos t-**N**-a sue bay-**BAY**
What's your baby's name?	¿Cómo se llama su bebé?	**CO**-mo say **YA**-ma sue bay-**BAY**
What pretty eyes!	¡Qué bonitos ojos!	kay bow-**KNEE**-toes **OH**-hoes

One for the Road: Phrases to Use Any Time

Obviously, conversation is made up of more than just lists of words. It will take practice and determination for you to achieve free-flowing conversation in a language that's new to you. Learning Spanish is a slow and steady process for adults. It could take several months before you begin to "think" in Spanish, so don't expect to achieve native speaker speed overnight! There will be times when you feel like you can't remember anything you've studied. That's natural. It happens to everyone. Try not to be discouraged. The rewards you'll receive from learning to speak Spanish are far greater than a little bit of frustration. If you keep working, it won't be long before you'll have a breakthrough. Learning Spanish is a lot like eating a great steak. You don't want to rush it. Cut each bite of your Spanish, chew it over carefully and savor each morsel. Moving along at a slower pace will help you retain what you learn longer.

Spanish is a language that has loads of zest and flair. It is punctuated with single words and short phrases that can really express a lot of sentiment. The next time you have an opportunity to observe native speakers, listen carefully. You may hear them switch from English to Spanish, depending on what they are saying. And, you might hear them use any of the phrases listed below. Expressions like these add spice to your conversation. Use the following list to help you take your Spanish conversational skills to the next level.

English	Español	Guide
Are you sure?	¿Está seguro? (a)	es-**TA** say-**GOO**-row
Excellent!	¡Excelente!	x-say-**LENT**-tay
Fantastic!	¡Fantástico!	fan-**TA**-stee-co
Good idea.	Buena idea.	boo-**A**-na e-**DAY**-ah
Happy birthday!	¡Feliz cumpleaños!	fay-**LEASE** coom-play-**AHN**-yos
Have a nice day.	Tenga un buen día.	**TEN**-ga un boo-**WAYNE DEE**-ah
I agree.	De acuerdo.	day ah-coo-**AIR**-doe
I believe so.	Creo que sí.	**CRAY**-oh kay **SEE**
I'm so glad.	Me alegro.	may ah-**LAY**-gro
I'll be right back.	¡Ahora vengo!	ah-**OR**-ah **VEIN**-go
I'm leaving now.	¡Ya me voy!	ya may **VOY**
That's OK.	Está bien.	es-**TA** b-**N**
It's important.	Es importante.	es eem-pour-**TAHN**-tay
It's serious.	Es grave.	es **GRA**-vay
It's possible.	Es posible	es po-**SEE**-blay
Like this?	¿Así?	ah-**SEE**
Maybe.	Quizás.	key-**SAHS**
Me, neither	Yo tampoco.	yo tam-**PO**-co
Me, too	Yo también.	yo tam-b-**N**
More or less	Más o menos.	mas oh **MAY**-nos
Really?	¿De veras?	day **VER**-ahs
Sure	¡Claro!	**CLA**-row
That depends.	Depende.	day-**PEN**-day
We'll see you.	Nos vemos.	nos **VAY**-mos

Typing in Spanish with Microsoft Word
Inserting an International Character with Shortcut Keys

When you need to type letters with accent marks or use Spanish punctuation, you will use keys that you have probably never used before! Actually, you are *composing characters* using the **control** key. It is located on the bottom row of keys. You will see that it is such an important key that there is one on both sides. It keeps the computer from moving forward one space so that the accent goes on *top* of the letter instead of *beside* it.

Always remember to hold the control key down first. It will be the *key* to your success in word processing Spanish. With a little practice these keys will become a normal part of your word processing skills.

Also, if using MS Word, you may use the menu command Insert>Symbol.

To insert	Press
á, é, í, ó, ú, ý Á, É, Í, Ó, Ú, Ý	CTRL+' (APOSTROPHE), *the letter*
â, ê, î, ô, û Â, Ê, Î, Ô, Û	CTRL+SHIFT+^ (CARET), *the letter*
ã, ñ, õ Ã, Ñ, Õ	CTRL+SHIFT+~ (TILDE), *the letter*
ä, ë, ï, ö, ü, ÿ Ä, Ë, Ï, Ö, Ü, Ÿ	CTRL+SHIFT+: (COLON), *the letter*
¿	ALT+CTRL+SHIFT+?
¡	ALT+CTRL+SHIFT+!

Practicing What You Have Learned

Practice is an important part of the language learning process. The more you include practice in your daily routine, the more comfortable and fluent you will become. There is no easy way to practice. It just takes time. The key to practicing Spanish is to set realistic goals. Don't let the language learning process become overwhelming to you. Yes, there is a lot to learn, and it will take some time. But, by setting realistic goals, you have a greater chance of sticking with it. Each of us have different learning styles, so find out what works best for you and break the material down into small pieces. Some of us learn best by listening. Others need to write the words and phrases in order to visualize them. Generally the more of your senses that you involve in the learning process, the faster you will retain the information. So, focus and practice one thing at a time. It's doing the little things that will make the greatest difference in the long run. Working five minutes every day on your Spanish is *mucho* better than trying to put in an hour of practice time only once each week. Consistency in your practice is critical.

Here are some practice tips that have worked for me and others who have participated in *SpeakEasy's Survival Spanish*™ training programs over the last few years.

1. Start practicing first thing in the morning. The shower is a great place to start. Say the numbers or run through the months of the year while you wash your hair. If you practice when you start your day you are more likely to continue to practice as the day progresses.

2. Use your commute time to practice. Listening to CDs, music and Spanish language radio stations will help you get the rhythm of Spanish. It will also increase your vocabulary.

3. If you are stopped in traffic, look around you for numbers on billboards or the license tags of the cars in front of you to help you practice. Don't just sit there—do something!

4. Investigate sites on the internet. Sites such as www.about.spanish.com and www.studyspanish.com are great places to practice and to learn, not to mention the fact that they are free!

5. Buy Spanish magazines or pick up Spanish newspapers that are published in your area. Many magazines like *People* have Spanish versions and almost every community in the country has a Spanish language newspaper or two. Many of them are free.

6. If there aren't any Spanish newspapers in your area, you can find a variety of publications from Latin America online. Major cities in Latin America all have newspapers that are easy to find on-line.

7. Practice as often as possible; even five minutes a day will help.

8. Don't give up! You didn't learn English overnight and you won't learn Spanish that way either. Set realistic goals and don't go too far too fast.

9. Learn five to ten words each week.

10. Practice at work with a friend.

11. Read! These books will make great additions to your library.

Baez, Francia and Chong, Nilda. *Latino Culture.* Intercultural Press, 2005

Condon, John. *Good Neighbors.* Intercultural Press, 1997

Einsohn, Marc and Steil, Gail. *The Idiot's Guide to Learning Spanish on Your Own.* Alpha Books, 1996

Harvey, William. *Spanish for Human Resource Managers.* Barron's, 1997

Hawson, Steven R. *Learn Spanish the Lazy Way.* Alpha Books, 1999.

Kras, Eva. *Management in Two Cultures.* Intercultural Press, 1995.

Reid, Elizabeth. Spanish *Lingo for the Savvy Gringo.* In One Ear Publications, 1997

Wald, Susana. *Spanish for Dummies.* Wiley Publishing, 2000.

Notes

Notes

About the Author

Myelita Melton

Myelita Melton, founder of SpeakEasy Communications, remembers the first time she heard a "foreign" language. She knew from that moment what she wanted to do with her life. "Since I was always the kid in class that talked too much," Myelita says, "I figured it would be a good idea to learn more than one language- that way I could talk to a lot more people!" After high school, she studied in Mexico at the *Instituto de Filológica Hispánica* and completed both her BA and MA in French and Curriculum Design at Appalachian State University in Boone, NC. She has studied and speaks five languages: French, Spanish, Italian, German, and English.

"Lita's" unique career includes classroom instruction and challenging corporate experience. She has won several national awards, including a prestigious *Rockefeller* scholarship. In 1994 she was named to *Who's Who Among Outstanding Americans*. Myelita's corporate experience includes owning a television production firm, working with NBC's Spanish news division, *Canal de Noticias,* and Charlotte's PBS affiliate WTVI. In her spare time, she continues to broadcast with WDAV, a National Public Radio affiliate near Lake Norman in North Carolina where she lives.

In 1997 Myelita started SpeakEasy Communications to offer industry specific Spanish instruction in North Carolina. The company is now the nation's leader in Spanish training, offering over 30 *SpeakEasy Spanish*™ programs and publications to companies, associations, and colleges throughout the US.

Lita is also a member of the National Speaker's Association and the National Council for Continuing Education and Training. Many of her clients say she is the most high-energy, results-oriented speaker they have ever seen. As she travels the country speaking on cultural diversity issues in the workplace and languages, she has truly realized her dream of being able to talk to the world.